New Directions for Student Services

Learning Communities from Start to Finish

Mimi Benjamin
EDITOR

Number 149 • Spring 2015
Jossey-Bass
San Francisco

Learning Communities from Start to Finish
Mimi Benjamin (ed.)
New Directions for Student Services, no. 149

Elizabeth J. Whitt, Editor-in-Chief
John H. Schuh, Associate Editor

New Directions for Student Services (ISSN 0164-7970, e-ISSN 1536-0695) is part of The Jossey-Bass Higher and Adult Education Series and is published quarterly by Wiley Subscription Services, Inc., A Wiley Company, at Jossey-Bass, One Montgomery Street, Suite 1200, San Francisco, CA 94104-4594. POSTMASTER: Send address changes to New Directions for Student Services, Jossey-Bass, One Montgomery Street, Suite 1200, San Francisco, CA 94104-4594.

New Directions for Student Services is indexed in CIJE: Current Index to Journals in Education (ERIC), Contents Pages in Education (T&F), Current Abstracts (EBSCO), Education Index /Abstracts (H.W. Wilson), Educational Research Abstracts Online (T&F), ERIC Database (Education Resources Information Center), and Higher Education Abstracts (Claremont Graduate University).

Microfilm copies of issues and articles are available in 16 mm and 35 mm, as well as microfiche in 105 mm, through University Microfilms Inc., 300 North Zeeb Road, Ann Arbor, Michigan 48106-1346.

Subscriptions cost $89 for individuals in the U.S., Canada, and Mexico, and $113 in the rest of the world for print only; $89 in all regions for electronic only; and $98 in the U.S., Canada, and Mexico for combined print and electronic; and $122 for combined print and electronic in the rest of the world. Institutional print only subscriptions are $335 in the U.S., $375 in Canada and Mexico, and $409 in the rest of the world; electronic only subscriptions are $335 in all regions; and combined print and electronic subscriptions are $402 in the U.S., $442 in Canada and Mexico, and $476 in the rest of the world.

Editorial correspondence should be sent to the Editor-in-Chief, Elizabeth J. Whitt, University of California Merced, 5200 North Lake Rd. Merced, CA 95343.

Cover design: Wiley
Cover Images: © Lava 4 images | Shutterstock

www.josseybass.com

CONTENTS

Editor's Notes

The pairing of the words "learning" and "community" speaks volumes about what we value and are trying to achieve through higher education. "Learning" is the primary mission of our institutions, and while the platforms for learning continue to evolve, we recognize that learning typically is not a solitary process. The element of "community" in our educational endeavors provides support, information, and opportunities to practice skills that are both academic and personal. By marrying these terms, we communicate and offer an opportunity for an educational experience that is supported and scaffolded by others.

Learning communities have been defined both broadly and more narrowly in the literature. Lenning, Hill, Saunders, Solan, and Stokes (2013) note the variety of groups for whom learning communities may be structured, including students and faculty/staff, as well as entire institutions. Cross (1998) defined them broadly to be composed of "groups of people engaged in intellectual interactions for the purpose of learning" (p. 4). A more narrow definition, provided by Smith, MacGregor, Matthews, and Gabelnick (2004), identified learning communities as "a variety of curricular approaches that intentionally link or cluster two or more courses, often around an interdisciplinary theme or problem, and enroll a common cohort of students" (p. 20), noting that residential programs include an integration of academic and out-of-class experiences. Lenning and others (2013) define student learning communities as "small groups of students intentionally organized (structurally and process-wise) for student–student, student–faculty, and student–curriculum interactions that will enhance student learning both for the group as a whole and for individual members of the group" (p. 7). Student learning communities are the focus of this volume, which provides historical, theoretical, and practical information for learning community work. These programs have been hailed as a valuable curricular structure and noted as a "high impact practice" (Kuh, 2008) for higher education.

Learning communities provide a specified community that can assist students in their integration into a college/university setting. *Powerful Partnerships: A Shared Responsibility for Learning* (American Association for Higher Education, American College Personnel Association, & National Association of Student Personnel Administrators, 1998) states, "Learning is fundamentally about making and maintaining connections: biologically through neural networks; mentally among concepts, ideas, and meanings; and experientially through interaction between the mind and the environment, self and other, generality and context, deliberation and action" (p. 5). Learning communities capitalize on these inherent connections that

New Directions for Student Services, no. 149, Spring 2015 © 2015 Wiley Periodicals, Inc.
Published online in Wiley Online Library (wileyonlinelibrary.com) • DOI: 10.1002/ss.20112

allow students to connect more closely with peers, faculty, staff, and academic material, reflecting a seamless learning experience that offers a holistic approach to students' educational experience. For those interested in implementing learning communities, this volume attempts to offer a starting point for information; experienced learning community faculty and staff may find the examples of and suggestions for successful program elements valuable in their continued learning community work.

Chapter 1 of this volume elaborates on the history of learning programs, forms of which have been created and modified since the early days of U.S. higher education. John E. Fink and Karen Kurotsuchi Inkelas overview the progression of learning community programs, from colonial times to present. They highlight various learning community structures and leave us to ponder what the next iteration of these programs will look like.

Jody Jessup-Anger provides an important theoretical overview of learning communities in Chapter 2. She notes long-standing formats for learning communities as well as more recent iterations of these programs and how theory informs the different approaches. Taking into consideration the history of these learning initiatives, she highlights the most recent as well as the foundational theoretical elements to be considered in the construction and implementation of learning communities.

With a particular focus on the students in these programs, John E. Fink and Mary L. Hummel identify inclusive approaches for coordinating learning communities in Chapter 3, responding to general concerns about providing quality experiences for underserved students. Their review of the literature resulted in a framework of "core practices of inclusive learning communities," a framework that can be implemented by any learning community program.

Jennifer R. Leptien's Chapter 4 provides readers with a view of learning communities from a different perspective—that of the learning community coordinator. Through this chapter, readers will have access to the experiences and ideas of professionals coordinating learning communities specifically for transfer students. Leptien's qualitative research provides both the voices of the coordinators along with recommendations for programs specifically for the transfer student population.

In Chapter 5, Daniel W. Calhoun and Lucy Santos Green offer suggestions for incorporating online learning communities into the list of learning community structures. In response to the proliferation of technological options available for pedagogical use, Calhoun and Green provide techniques and tools for programs offered in an online format. The authors offer a thorough overview of ways to make use of the online environment to structure programs, spotlighting the importance of "community" in these learning communities resulting from active engagement between students and their fellow learning community members.

Many learning community programs take advantage of the benefits of upper-division peers to assist learning community participants. Not all programs employ peer mentors, but peer mentor programs can be a valuable asset to learning community programs. Laura Jo Rieske and I identify elements of existing peer mentor programs and make suggestions when considering the implementation of a learning community peer mentor program in Chapter 6.

In order to demonstrate that learning communities are worth the time, effort, and resources dedicated to the programs, assessment is critical. In Chapter 7, Ann M. Gansemer-Topf and Kari Tietjen offer an example of an assessment focused on student learning. Highlighting the learning experiences of women participating in the Program for Women in Science and Engineering (PWSE) at Iowa State University, the authors provide both outcomes information and an assessment structure that may be useful to those coordinating learning community assessment elsewhere.

Finally, Sarah Conte's annotated bibliography, which serves as Chapter 8, summarizes recent literature on learning community programs. This valuable addition to the sourcebook will be helpful to professionals working with learning communities who are seeking research and literature in order to incorporate new information and ideas for their learning community work.

While not an exhaustive review of all things related to learning communities, this volume does provide valuable information for and examples of working with learning communities "from start to finish"—from the conceptualization stage that naturally includes consideration of history and theory to the assessment stage that provides the feedback necessary to improve the programs. I hope that you find this volume useful, whether you are a highly experienced learning communities professional or just beginning your journey with these programs.

Mimi Benjamin
Editor

References

American Association for Higher Education, American College Personnel Association, & National Association of Student Personnel Administrators. (1998). *Powerful partnerships: A shared responsibility for learning*. Washington, DC: Author.

Cross, K. P. (1998). Why learning communities? Why now? *About Campus*, 3(3), 4–11.

Kuh, G. D. (2008). *High-impact educational practices: What they are, who has access to them, and why they matter*. Washington, DC: Association of American Colleges and Universities.

Lenning, O. T., Hill, D. M., Saunders, K. P., Solan, A., & Stokes, A. (2013). *Powerful learning communities: A guide to developing student, faculty and professional learning communities to improve student success and organizational effectiveness*. Sterling, VA: Stylus.

Smith, B. L., MacGregor, J., Matthews, R. S., & Gabelnick, F. (2004). *Learning communities: Reforming undergraduate education*. San Francisco, CA: Wiley.

MIMI BENJAMIN is an assistant professor in the Student Affairs in Higher Education Department at Indiana University of Pennsylvania.

1

This chapter describes the historical development of learning communities within American higher education. We examine the forces both internal and external to higher education that contributed to and stalled the emergence of learning communities in their contemporary form.

A History of Learning Communities Within American Higher Education

John E. Fink, Karen Kurotsuchi Inkelas

Learning communities have become prominent throughout the course of U.S. higher education history. In their contemporary form, learning communities have commonly been defined as "curricular linkages that provide students with a deeper examination and integration of themes or concepts that they are learning" (Gabelnick, MacGregor, Matthews, & Smith, 1990; Shapiro & Levine, 1999, as cited in Inkelas & Soldner, 2012, p. 2). Using this definition, we describe the historical evolution of learning communities in the United States from the early colonial colleges through the 21st century. Ultimately, the evolution of learning communities and their role within higher education were based upon forces both internal and external to higher education. The contemporary definition of a learning community encompasses residential and nonresidential types, yet the residential model was most prominent in the early history of learning communities within the United States. Thus, we begin with the history of residential learning communities.

"Oxbridge" Residential College Model

Colonial influence established learning communities as a central facet of the American college experience at the conception of U.S. higher education. Chaddock (2008) argued that one motive for establishing the early American colleges "was to plant British culture and intellect on the rugged and raw terrain of the infant colonies" (p. 10). Therefore, founders of several American colleges drew upon two prominent English universities, Oxford and Cambridge. This "Oxbridge" inspiration included a residential college model that was the precursor to contemporary living-learning programs. Colleges such as Harvard, Princeton, William and Mary, and Yale followed

New Directions for Student Services, no. 149, Spring 2015 © 2015 Wiley Periodicals, Inc.
Published online in Wiley Online Library (wileyonlinelibrary.com) • DOI: 10.1002/ss.20113

the Oxbridge residential college model by colocating students' sleeping quarters, dining halls, lecture halls, tutor residences, and common areas. Intent on molding students' whole selves, students and their tutors lived, worked, studied, and socialized together as a part of the residential college model. Despite debate on the extent to which the Oxbridge residential college model was precisely replicated in the early colonial colleges, the Oxbridge model has sustained significance for contemporary discussion of learning communities (Inkelas & Soldner, 2012).

While the Oxbridge residential college model was a core component at some institutions, the residential college model did not initially flourish in U.S. higher education. Chaddock (2008) argued that, around the turn of the 19th century, the growth in student population and the questionable value of integrating academic and residential life contributed to a departure from the Oxbridge residential college ideal. For example, in order to accommodate larger numbers of students, Harvard and Yale built dormitories that deviated from the residential college model. Furthermore, the passage of the Morrill Land Grant Act of 1862 coincided with the growing importance of discipline-focused graduate training and research production for faculty members. Despite the central role residential colleges played in early American higher education, the rise of the research university and its Germanic model of higher education in the 19th century precluded the residential college model from retaining prominence amid the expanding landscape.

Foundational Reformers in the 20th Century

Critiques of the Germanic model of higher education from within the academy created internal pressure for learning communities to regain prominence at the turn of the 20th century. Educational philosophers John Dewey and Alexander Meiklejohn provided substantive critiques of the Germanic model of higher education, and in doing so laid the philosophical foundation for the contemporary learning community movement. John Dewey valued students' holistic development, and he critiqued the Germanic model of higher education as not fully engaging students with their learning. Dewey believed that learning should be active and collaborative where students drive their own discovery. Ideal learning environments from Dewey's perspective would take place in both academic and cocurricular settings, as well as situating learning as "shared inquiry" between students and teachers rather than the one-way transfer of knowledge from expert to student (Smith, MacGregor, Matthews, & Gabelnick, 2004). Furthermore, as a pragmatist, Dewey critiqued educational institutions as being too divorced from society. In his calls for education reform, Dewey claimed that student learning ideally should be experiential, applied, and connected to societal problems (Nelson, 2001).

Meiklejohn departed from Dewey in his perspective on the role of educational institutions within society. Throughout his tenure as president at

Amherst College during World War I, Meiklejohn deepened his conviction that "First [and foremost], the college should be withdrawn from the world of affairs in order to remain entirely unbiased" (Meiklejohn, as cited in Nelson, 2001, p. 95). Meiklejohn also problematized the rise of the Germanic model of higher education and subsequent intellectual fragmentation into distinct academic disciplines. Specifically, Meiklejohn critiqued the increasingly prevalent elective system as too incoherent. He foresaw the challenge to general education presented by the Germanic model and instead sought an integrated core curriculum for students (Smith et al., 2004). Critiquing higher education from within the academy, Dewey and Meiklejohn initially situated learning communities as powerful tools for educational reform.

Leaving Amherst, Meiklejohn sought a new educational setting to apply his vision of the ideal college and founded the Experimental College at the University of Wisconsin in 1927. Described as the "progenitor of the modern living-learning program" (Inkelas & Soldner, 2012, p. 14), the Experimental College played a key role in learning community history despite its brief existence from 1927 to 1932. Both the content and process of learning were innovative in the Experimental College. Contrasting the prevalent elective system, students took a two-year common curriculum focused on democracy and classical Western thought. Furthermore, students engaged in the educative process in more active and collaborative ways that contrasted with that of their fellow university students. For example, students learned through team-taught and clustered courses, as well as shared residences and dining facilities. Assigned to students to complete in the summer between their first and second years, the "Regional Study" project challenged students to investigate how their hometowns operated as democracies. This project exemplified the active and experiential nature of learning within the Experimental College. Students also formed clubs, such as the Philosophy and Law clubs, to extend the learning environment beyond their coursework (Nelson, 2001; Smith et al., 2004). However, after just five years, the Experimental College's drastically different expectations of students, compensation of faculty, and curricular design garnered campus criticism, and it subsequently closed. Yet, Meiklejohn's use of a learning community model as an attempt at reform within higher education, particularly at large research universities, was echoed in the rise of the learning community movement in the latter half of the 20th century.

Learning Community Innovation Amid Post-WWII Expansion

The substantial increase in the amount and diversity of students seeking higher education after passage of the WWII G.I. Bill was another key influence in the history of learning communities. To meet the demands of the larger and more diverse population of students seeking postsecondary education, a range of different types of institutions developed in the 20th century. At the time, land grant universities and small, liberal arts colleges were common, but new types of institutions such as junior colleges, community colleges, technical schools, teachers colleges, regional institutions, and minority-serving institutions developed to meet growing demands for postsecondary education (Thelin, 2003). Furthermore, the growth in number and diversity of both students and institutions after WWII yielded later scrutiny of educational quality. Once again internal reformers experimented with learning communities to address questions of higher educational quality. Smith and others (2004) described a small group of academics, inspired by previous reformers like Meiklejohn, who created multiple innovations to promote quality undergraduate education. Among these were innovations at the University of California, San Jose State, LaGuardia Community College, and Stony Brook, and the creation of Evergreen State College. These reformers, Smith et al. argued, brought forth the contemporary learning community movement. The following sections describe a few prominent examples of these internal reforms in the second half of the 20th century.

Tussman's Learning Community at Berkeley. A protégé of Meiklejohn's, Joseph Tussman developed a learning community at UC Berkeley, similar to Meiklejohn's Experimental College, which provided an interdisciplinary, two-year curriculum aimed at preparing students to be democratic citizens. Students learned through self-guided study and writing-intensive team-taught courses, and the learning community also enjoyed a distinct physical space that supported the creation of community. Despite only existing from 1965 to 1969, Tussman's learning community reflected his belief that undergraduate education should focus on democratic participation, even at large research universities. As a critic of higher education, Tussman noted years after the Berkeley learning community was suspended, "The fundamental delusion may have been to suppose that it was possible for a great organism like the university to sustain for long an enterprise so at odds with its essential nature" (Tussman, as cited in Smith et al., 2004, p. 42). The tension between undergraduate student learning and research production, central to Tussman's critique of higher education, maintains relevance in contemporary learning community initiatives.

Early Learning Community Initiatives. Multiple learning community initiatives took form in the 1960s and 1970s during and following Tussman's experiment at Berkeley. Simultaneous to Tussman, Mervyn Cadwallader created a similar learning community at San Jose State in California. In fact, as Smith et al. (2004) noted, Cadwallader, Tussman, and Meiklejohn interacted multiple times in the 1960s, exchanging ideas and planning contemporary versions of the Experimental College. Similarly, Cadwallader's learning community only lasted from 1965 to 1969, encountering many of the same challenges as did the learning community at Berkeley. Cadwallader again endeavored to implement his educational reforms at the State University of New York–Old Westbury but was unsuccessful as the university was in turmoil and closed shortly after Cadwallader arrived.

However, other reformers on the east coast began to form learning communities around the same time. Roberta Matthews was an associate dean at LaGuardia Community College interested in fostering collaborative, interdisciplinary education at community colleges. Under her leadership, LaGuardia established a learning clusters model wherein students coenrolled in multiple, similar courses with coordinated curricula. Faculty teams at LaGuardia Community College carefully aligned their curricula to provide an integrated learning experience for students. Meanwhile, Patrick Hill, a philosophy professor at State University of New York–Stony Brook, launched a federated learning community initiative at Stony Brook. Hill is noteworthy for resurfacing the term "learning community" and for translating the learning community model to research universities. In Hill's federated learning communities, students would coenroll in two existing university courses and a third integrative seminar. Alongside the cohort of students taking these three courses would be a faculty member, called the "master learner," who also took the courses and directed the integrative seminar. The federated learning community model reflected Hill's philosophy as a pragmatist in creating institutional change, as well as his way to address the enduring challenge of creating environments supportive of quality undergraduate education at research universities (Smith et al., 2004).

Evergreen State College. In the 1970s, multiple educational reformers organized as the founding faculty of the Evergreen State College in Washington. Creating a new institution allowed the founders to agree at the outset on the educational philosophy and structure of the college. The influence of Tussman and Meiklejohn was clear, Smith et al. (2004) argued, as Mervyn Cadwallader played a key role among the founding faculty members. From the founding of the college, everyone committed to team-taught, yearlong programs of study, and this structure was supported by other college policies such as faculty merit and organizational structure. Cadwallader was an influential early dean who sought to establish a Meiklejohn- and Tussman-inspired curriculum focused on preparing students as citizens for democracy. As the college developed, the pedagogies and teaching styles of Dewey, Meiklejohn, and Tussman remained central, but the content of coursework successfully expanded to a variety of topics. Evergreen State College has long since served as a leader in the contemporary learning community movement within higher education (Smith et al., 2004).

The Late 20th Century and the Era of Accountability in Higher Education

The 1980s and 1990s were marked by increasingly fervent calls for reform in U.S. undergraduate education. Eerily echoing the same allegations made by Dewey and Meiklejohn nearly a century earlier, critics described undergraduate education—especially at large public research universities—as too passive, disconnected, incoherent, and disengaging. Several policy agencies and organizations issued reports identifying U.S. undergraduate education's shortfalls, including the National Institute of Education (NIE). In *Involvement in Learning: Realizing the Potential of American Higher Education* (NIE, 1984), the NIE called for U.S. colleges and universities to center their undergraduate educational opportunities on student learning. They advocated for institutions to (a) organize smaller communities of learning; (b) provide more formal and informal ways for faculty and students to interact more frequently with themselves and one another; and (c) integrate their curricula to be more inclusive, coherent, and connected.

From 1996 to 2000, the Kellogg Commission on the Future of State and Land-Grant Universities (2001) produced six reports in a series entitled *Returning to Our Roots*, in which they provided key recommendations to public and land-grant institutions regarding systemic change in public higher education. Providing similar descriptions of undergraduate education as were in *Involvement in Learning*, the Kellogg Commission added that undergraduate enrollment at large public universities has increased and continues to increase, and that the new enrollments are increasingly diverse by racial/ethnic, socioeconomic, and college preparation backgrounds. At the same time, partly due to declines in state support for public higher education, undergraduate tuition has experienced a sharp increase, often at rates higher than other economic indicators.

Added to this dire picture was the growing fear that American education (K–16) was not preparing its youth to compete in the global economy. In 1983, the United States National Commission on Excellence in Education published *A Nation at Risk: The Imperative for Educational Reform*, which alleged that the U.S. educational system was failing to produce a globally competitive workforce. Taken together, then, U.S. undergraduate education—especially at large public universities—was taking in more undergraduates than ever, charging increasingly higher tuition, and delivering a subpar education that would not provide its graduates the necessary skills to compete in the global economy.

This combination of phenomena has resulted in an erosion of public trust, and has forced American higher education to create and institute new and improved ways to deliver its undergraduate education. Beginning in the 1980s and continuing to present day, state governments and accreditation agencies are requiring colleges and universities to account for the quality of their undergraduate experience, including information regarding access and retention, evidence of educational excellence, and justification for their costs. Simultaneously, parents and students are demanding to know what their tuition pays for, and exactly what will be the return on their investment (Harper, Sax, & Wolf, 2012).

Learning Communities as a Reform Effort. Many of the same reports chastising the current state of undergraduate education also provided recommendations for how institutions could improve their efforts, and many of them advocated for the creation of learning communities. The NIE

(1984) asserted that institutions needed to create smaller, more intimate learning spaces for students: "Every institution of higher education should strive to create learning communities, organized around specific intellectual themes or tasks" (p. 35). The Kellogg Commission on the Future of State and Land-Grant Universities (1997) similarly ended its *Returning to Our Roots: The Student Experience* report calling for public and land-grant institutions to create learning communities.

More recently, in 2008, the Association of American Colleges and Universities released a report entitled *High-Impact Educational Practices: What They Are, Who Has Access to Them, and Why They Matter* (Kuh, 2008). In it, George Kuh, using data from the National Survey of Student Engagement (NSSE) and elsewhere, identified 10 postsecondary educational practices found empirically to confer substantial benefits to students and their college performance and retention. Included in the 10 practices are learning communities, but also included are first-year seminars and common intellectual experiences, which also could be construed as part of a broader definition of learning communities.

Types of Learning Communities. Given increasing demands by external stakeholders for undergraduate education accountability as well as explicit directives from policymakers on how to improve it, it is not surprising that so many U.S. colleges and universities—particularly large public research universities—took the advice of these policy organizations and created different forms of learning communities on their campuses. Smith et al. (2004) reported that by 2000, more than 500 institutions of different types and controls had established learning communities. Some campuses had even begun to require learning community participation as part of their general education program. Learning communities are now so ubiquitous on American college and university campuses that they have their own category in the *U.S. News and World Report* rankings.

While there is no professional organization uniting individuals or campuses involved with learning communities, the Washington Center for Improving the Quality of Undergraduate Education at Evergreen State College has emerged as the *de facto* leader in the learning community movement. Through funding from the Washington state legislature, the Exxon Foundation, and the Ford Foundation, the Washington Center now serves as a support system for learning community efforts around the United States, promoting the sharing of information regarding learning community assessment data, promising practices, and implementation strategies (Smith et al., 2004; Washington Center at The Evergreen State College, 2013).

Along with the expansion in popularity of learning communities arose an expansion in our understanding of what constitutes a learning community. Over the years, several authors have constructed various typologies of learning communities, including Gabelnick et al. (1990), Shapiro and Levine (1999), Lenning and Ebbers (1999), Smith et al. (2004), and Lenning, Hill, Saunders, Stokes, and Solan (2013), as well as Inkelas,

Soldner, Longerbeam, and Leonard's (2008) empirical typology of residential learning communities, also known as living-learning programs. Inkelas and Soldner (2012) combined these various typologies into one master typology and suggested the following as an integrated model:

1. Paired or clustered courses.
2. Smaller cohorts among large enrollments, including FIGs and federated learning communities.
3. Coordinated or team-taught series of courses.
4. Learning communities for special populations (for example, women in STEM majors).
5. Residentially based learning communities. (p. 7)

These five types likely represent the most dominant forms of learning communities found on American college and university campuses today. But what is to come? What does the future hold for learning communities? Similar to its history, the future of learning communities will no doubt be shaped by external forces that higher education can no longer afford to ignore.

The Next Crossroad: Online and Technology-Infused Education

Anyone following U.S. higher education today knows that technology has forever changed the landscape of college teaching and the curriculum. Recently, the Massive Open Online Course, or MOOC, gained so much media coverage that the *New York Times* named 2012 the "Year of the MOOC." However, MOOCs are just one type of mechanism through which technology has been infused in teaching and learning in American higher education. Harasim (2000) describes three primary modes of educational delivery using technology: (a) adjunct mode, (b) mixed mode, and (c) online mode. Adjunct mode is best characterized by an instructor's use of technology-enhanced support for various course functions (using email to communicate outside of class, administering online tests or examinations, etc.), but the traditional, in-class component remains the primary source of instruction. Mixed, or hybrid, mode involves using online components for a significant portion of a traditional course, so much so that in-class instruction is significantly altered. One of the more popular versions of the mixed mode is the "flipped classroom," in which instructors deliver the lecture online via video and/or additional readings, thereby freeing up in-person class time to do more active learning types of activities, such as problem solving, case studies, and/or peer learning. Finally, the online mode uses the web or computer network as the primary vehicle for the course, with no in-person class component. More classic forms of distance learning such as virtual classrooms, as well as MOOCs, would be classified under this mode.

All three modes of technology-infused delivery systems raise new challenges for the notion of the learning community. Recalling that early *and* contemporary critics described undergraduate education as passive, impersonal, and disconnected, how do technological innovations that replace more and more of the in-person classroom function serve to change, or even eliminate, the concept of a community of learners? To be sure, MOOCs that can enroll more than 100,000 individuals in a single course stretch even the most imaginative boundaries of how the term "learning community" can be defined. What kind of faculty–student interaction in a MOOC is even possible with that many students? What online mechanisms must be created and cultivated in a MOOC to encourage peer collaboration in a class of that size? How do students achieve *depth* of learning in a course where content delivery is as asynchronous as a web format when anyone who registers for a MOOC class can view the course material at any time, in any place, and in any manner of choosing?

Yet, challenges to the learning community concept are not only germane to the MOOC. Even in the adjunct mode of delivery, we know little about how learning communities may be formed when the class utilizes blogs or discussion boards. For example, how can we ensure that diverse voices are heard in an online discussion board? How do we prevent students from reposting blog or discussion board comments to an external forum and thereby possibly destroying the sense of trust that is so critical in building a learning community? In the mixed mode, similar challenges may arise. For example, how do we successfully blend the content introduced in the online materials with the in-class discussions to create optimal learning environments? How do we create a different kind of learning climate in a classroom that may now be 100% based on active and collaborative learning practices when some students may not be accustomed to or comfortable in such a setting? Needless to say, there is much left to be studied when it comes to technology-infused education and learning communities.

Conclusion

Contemporary undergraduate education is an amalgamation of all of the forms of learning communities we have described in this short history. There are still plenty of examples of the Oxbridge model of residential colleges in existence, particularly at some of the nation's most elite institutions. As mentioned previously, there are over 500 learning communities currently in operation in postsecondary institutions around the country, representing all forms in the learning community typology. And, now, with adjunct, mixed, and online versions of technology-rich courses, we have an ever-evolving notion of the 21st-century learning community. Each of these forms of learning communities resulted from internal or external forces placing pressure on American higher education to change its practices—whether the pressure was to conform to British standards for educational quality, to make student learning more active and participatory, to educate a democratic citizenry, to account for increasing enrollments and tuition amid questions concerning a college education's value, or to adapt to technological advancements that revolutionize the sharing of information worldwide. What does the future hold, and what new pressures will bring to bear even greater changes in the learning community landscape? Only time will tell.

References

Chaddock, K. E. (2008). From inventions of necessity to necessary invention: The evolution of learning in residential settings. In G. Luna & J. Gahagan (Eds.), *Learning initiatives in the residential setting* (pp. 7–17). Columbia, SC: National Resource Center for the First-Year Experience and Students in Transition, University of South Carolina.

Gabelnick, F., MacGregor, J., Matthews, R. S., & Smith, B. L. (Eds.). (1990). *New Directions for Teaching and Learning: No. 41. Learning communities: Creating connections among students, faculty, and disciplines*. San Francisco, CA: Jossey-Bass.

Harasim, L. (2000). Shift happens: Online education as a new paradigm in learning. *Internet and Higher Education*, *3*(1), 41–61.

Harper, C. E., Sax, L. J., & Wolf, D. S. (2012). The role of parents in college students' sociopolitical awareness, academic, and social development. *Journal of Student Affairs Research and Practice*, *49*(2), 137–156.

Inkelas, K. K., & Soldner, M. (2012). Undergraduate living-learning programs and student outcomes. In J. C. Smart & M. B. Paulsen (Eds.), *Higher education: Handbook of theory and research* (Vol. 26, pp. 1–55). New York, NY: Springer.

Inkelas, K. K., Soldner, M., Longerbeam, S., & Leonard, J. (2008). Differences in student outcomes by types of living-learning programs: The development of an empirical typology. *Research in Higher Education*, *49*(6), 495–512.

Kellogg Commission on the Future of State and Land-Grant Universities. (1997). *Returning to our roots: The student experience*. Washington, DC: National Association of State Universities and Land Grant Colleges.

Kellogg Commission on the Future of State and Land-Grant Universities. (2001). *Returning to our roots: Executive summaries of the reports of the Kellogg Commission on the future of state and land-grant universities*. Washington, DC: National Association of State Universities and Land Grant Colleges.

Kuh, G. D. (2008). *High-impact educational practices: What they are, who has access to them, and why they matter*. Washington, DC: Association of American Colleges and Universities.

Lenning, O. T., & Ebbers, L. H. (1999). *The powerful potential of learning communities: Improving education for the future* (ASHE-ERIC Higher Education Report, 26[6]). Washington, DC: Graduate School of Education and Human Development, The George Washington University.

Lenning, O. T., Hill, D. M., Saunders, K. P., Stokes, A., & Solan, A. (2013). *Powerful learning communities: A guide to developing student, faculty, and professional learning communities to improve student success and organizational effectiveness*. Sterling, VA: Stylus.

National Institute of Education (NIE). (1984). *Involvement in learning: Realizing the potential of American higher education. Final report of the study group on the conditions of excellence in American higher education* (Stock No. 065-000-00213-2). Washington, DC: U.S. Government Printing Office.

Nelson, A. (2001). *Education and democracy: The meaning of Alexander Meiklejohn, 1872–1964*. Madison, WI: University of Wisconsin Press.

Shapiro, N. S., & Levine, J. H. (1999). *Creating learning communities: A practical guide to winning support, organizing for change, and implementing programs*. San Francisco, CA: Jossey-Bass.

Smith, B. L., MacGregor, J., Matthews, R. S., & Gabelnick, F. (2004). *Learning communities: Reforming undergraduate education*. San Francisco, CA: Wiley.

Thelin, J. R. (2003). Historical overview of American higher education. In S. R. Komives & D. Woodard, Jr. (Eds.), *Student services: A handbook for the profession* (4th ed., pp. 3–22). San Francisco, CA: Jossey-Bass.

United States National Commission on Excellence in Education. (1983). *A nation at risk: The imperative for educational reform. A report to the nation and the Secretary of Education, United States Department of Education*. Washington, DC: Author.

Washington Center at The Evergreen State College. (2013). *About the center*. Retrieved from http://www.evergreen.edu/washingtoncenter/about/index.html

JOHN E. FINK coordinates the Transfer2Terp Learning Community in the Adele H. Stamp Student Union at the University of Maryland.

KAREN KUROTSUCHI INKELAS is associate professor and director of the Center for Advanced Study of Teaching and Learning in Higher Education at the University of Virginia.

2

This chapter describes the historical and contemporary theoretical underpinnings of learning communities and argues that there is a need for more complex models in conceptualizing and assessing their effectiveness.

Theoretical Foundations of Learning Communities

Jody E. Jessup-Anger

Over the past half century, learning communities have evolved from an innovation adopted in isolation by postsecondary institutions to a widespread reform movement embraced by over 800 colleges and universities (Matthews, Smith, & MacGregor, 2012). Scholars describe a learning community as "an intentionally developed community that exists to promote and maximize the individual and shared learning of its members. There is ongoing interaction, interplay, and collaboration among the community's members as they strive for specified common learning goals" (Lenning, Hill, Saunders, Solan, & Stokes, 2013, p. 7). More specifically, learning communities arrange the curriculum to promote coherence in students' learning and increase intellectual interaction with faculty and peers (Gabelnick, MacGregor, Matthews, & Smith, 1990). The structure of a learning community can vary widely, from pairing courses from different disciplines with a common theme (e.g., a sociology and psychology course on poverty) to more tightly coordinated studies that may encompass the entire educational experience during a given semester for both students and faculty (Matthews, Smith, MacGregor, & Gabelnick, 1997). Some learning communities incorporate a residential component into their design as well (Shapiro & Levine, 1999).

The growth of learning communities is linked to broader reforms in undergraduate education that emerged as a result of concerns about the quality of undergraduate education detailed in reports by the Association of American Colleges (1985), the Boyer Commission on Educating Undergraduates in the Research University (1998), the Wingspread Group on Higher Education (1993), and the Association of American Colleges and Universities (AAC&U) (2002). These reports raised concerns about undergraduate student learning and retention, as well as the content and coherence of the curriculum. More recently, the identification of learning

NEW DIRECTIONS FOR STUDENT SERVICES, no. 149, Spring 2015 © 2015 Wiley Periodicals, Inc.
Published online in Wiley Online Library (wileyonlinelibrary.com) • DOI: 10.1002/ss.20114

communities as a research-based "high-impact practice" (AAC&U, 2007; Kuh, 2008) has bolstered interest in developing, sustaining, and assessing learning communities. Given the continuing interest in learning communities, this chapter provides an overview of their historical theoretical foundations, the research that undergirds their structure, and contemporary frameworks useful in conceptualizing and understanding their impact.

Historic Theoretical Roots of Learning Communities

As indicated in the previous chapter, most scholars credit educational theorists Alexander Meiklejohn and John Dewey (Gabelnick et al., 1990; Lenning & Ebbers, 1999) with providing the structural foundation of contemporary learning communities in the United States. Whereas contemporary educators laud Meiklejohn for his structural contribution to learning communities, they credit John Dewey with envisioning the pedagogical foundations, specifically "student-centered learning and active learning," two concepts espoused by contemporary learning community advocates (Gabelnick et al., 1990, p. 15). Dewey encouraged educators to ground the curriculum in students' experiences, cultivating students' individuality, advancing their interests, and promoting their construction of knowledge (Dewey, 1938). Although he was focused on the learning experience, Dewey stressed the importance of maintaining subject matter at the center of education, emphasizing that content should drive the teaching method and arguing that the outcome of a successful educational experience is an expanded understanding of subject matter coupled with an acknowledgment that there is more to know (Dewey, 1916). In a learning community environment, Dewey's ideas have been advanced by examining big questions and using differing disciplinary perspectives to illustrate the complexity of these questions, encouraging students to seek out further knowledge. Because Dewey's work focused more on primary and secondary schooling than on postsecondary education (Dewey, 1916, 1938, 1974), the application of his ideas in collegiate learning communities is fraught with difficulty, as one teacher is not the sole conductor of students' educational experiences. Rather, a learning community may include several instructors, academic advisors, and sometimes residence life staff or other administrators. These individuals may have varying levels of understanding of and commitment to the subject matter of the course or courses, may not see the connections across disciplines, and tend to view one another with suspicion (Golde & Pribbenow, 2000). Thus, constant coordination and communication are critical to a successful learning community environment, which may explain in part why early learning communities were fleeting.

Theoretical and Research Support for Learning Communities

Since the mid-1980s, learning communities have flourished in a variety of postsecondary contexts. Student development theory and research support the aims and outcomes of these communities. Below are several theories and research studies that support the learning community structure. For a comprehensive overview of the cognitive theory that supports the learning community design, readers should refer to *Powerful Learning Communities: A Guide to Developing Student, Faculty and Professional Learning Communities to Improve Student Success and Organizational Effectiveness* (Lenning et al., 2013).

Astin's Involvement Theory. Among the conditions of the college environment that Astin (1984) maintains are critical to student development is involvement, which he defined as "the investment of physical and psychological energy in various objects" (p. 298). Astin argued that the amount of learning and development connected with an educational endeavor is proportional to the quality and quantity of student involvement in the experience and that some students will invest more energy than others in their educational activities. The structure of learning communities, with paired classes and intentional activities to foster faculty and peer interaction, is well suited to increase student involvement and thus enhance development.

Tinto's Departure Theory. Vincent Tinto's (1993) work on student departure led to his interest in and research on the effectiveness of learning communities (Tinto, Goodsell Love, & Russo, 1994) in promoting student persistence. In his theory of individual departure, Tinto contends that students' decisions to leave a postsecondary institution stem from the interaction between their individual attributes (skills, prior educational experiences, and dispositions) and the academic and social systems of the institution (Tinto, 1993). He stressed the importance of academic and social integration into the institution, arguing that those students who choose to leave a postsecondary institution often do so because they are not academically or socially connected to the institution (Tinto, 1993). In research conducted at both two- and four-year institutions, Tinto and others found that students in learning communities form their own supportive peer groups that provide academic and social support, are more actively involved in classroom learning even after class, and ultimately learn more (Tinto et al., 1994). Looking more specifically at living-learning communities, Wawrzynski, Jessup-Anger, Helman, Stolz, and Beaulieu (2009) had similar findings, namely that these communities produced a culture that promoted seamless learning, a scholarly environment, and an ethos of relatedness among faculty and peers.

Interdisciplinary Studies. Alexander Meiklejohn's belief in and promotion of interdisciplinary studies, coupled with his influence on the learning community movement via the Experimental College, in part explain the influence of interdisciplinary studies on the learning community movement. Although there is variation in the definition, broadly speaking, interdisciplinary studies are defined as "a process of answering a question, solving a problem, or addressing a topic that is too broad or complex to be dealt with adequately by a single discipline or profession" (Klein & Newell, 1997, p. 393). Often learning communities take an interdisciplinary approach in their curricular design, pairing students with two or more courses with similar topics from different disciplines. For example, among the offerings at Skagit Valley Community College in Mount Vernon, WA, is a learning community entitled *Composing the American Diet*, which pairs an English composition class and a nutrition class. The instructors of these classes agree to integrate their course topics and readings, discussing them from varying perspectives while also sharing assignments, readings, and activities. Although the interdisciplinary approach to a learning community requires faculty coordination and structural support, when it is done well, it can promote greater coherence and connectedness in the curriculum, ultimately improving student learning (Klein & Newell, 1997).

Learning Communities as a High-Impact Practice and Other Relevant Research. In 2007, the AAC&U identified learning communities as one of 10 effective educational practices. Kuh (2008) used data from the National Study of Student Engagement to illustrate the strong positive effect of participating in a learning community and other high-impact practices, noting that students who participated in these activities reported greater gains in learning and personal development. These findings echo those of other researchers (see Taylor, Moore, MacGregor, & Lindblad [2003] for a comprehensive review) who demonstrated that, overall, students who participate in learning communities have a richer academic experience; however, much of that richness is dependent on how the learning community is implemented. Lichtenstein (2005) found that the classroom environment plays an important role in the success of learning communities, with student outcomes varying greatly depending on the extent to which the classroom environment promoted linkages between classes, communication between faculty, and used active learning methods and out-of-class group experiences.

Cox and Orehovec (2007) also noted tremendous variation across learning community environments. Using data from their study of faculty–student interactions in living-learning community environments, Cox and Orehovec developed a typology detailing interactions ranging from disengagement to mentoring, with incidental contact, functional interaction, and personal interaction defining the middle of the continuum. The authors argued that even in a learning community environment, which is marked by an expectation that faculty and students will interact outside of class, the greatest type of interaction is disengagement, as often faculty and students have little common ground on which to build a relationship. The authors suggested examining the cultural norms of the institution to determine the value placed on faculty–student interaction.

Online Learning Communities. As detailed in Calhoun and Green's "Utilizing Online Learning Communities in Student Affairs" (Chapter 5 of this volume), the emergence and rapid growth of online learning have raised questions about the possibility of creating virtual communities that support the individual and shared learning of its members. Whereas in a traditional learning community the structure is such that students are likely to be physically present with one another regardless of if they interact, in an online community, if students are not actively engaged, it is as though they are not in class at all (Palloff & Pratt, 2007). Garrison, Anderson, and Archer (2000) developed the Community of Inquiry Framework, a model of the necessary elements for the development of community and pursuit of inquiry in an online environment. Included in the model are three interacting core elements: cognitive presence, social presence, and teaching presence. Cognitive presence addresses learners' construction and confirmation of meaning through reflection and discourse within the online community (Garrison & Anderson, 2003). Social presence addresses participants' ability to project themselves as "real people" in the virtual community. Finally, teaching presence encompasses "instructional management, building understanding, and direct instruction" (Garrison et al., 2000, p. 101). As one might expect, the elements necessary for a virtual community to flourish are similar to those in traditional learning communities.

The aforementioned studies illustrate that the mere presence of a learning community does not ensure positive learning outcomes, and attention needs to be paid to how learning communities are implemented. Wawrzynski and Jessup-Anger's (2010) longitudinal research on the effect of resource allocation to learning-community environments supports this claim. They found that the organizational structure of the environment affected students' academic experiences. Specifically, students who were in more comprehensively resourced communities—those with faculty affiliated directly with the community, classes or sections of classes geared to students in the community, and blended student and academic affairs roles within the community—reported significantly higher levels of academic peer interactions and perceived their environment as academically rich.

Contemporary Frameworks for Conceptualizing and Assessing Learning Communities—Ecology Theory

As illustrated earlier, designing and assessing learning community environments are difficult because of the myriad different aspects to attend to, including instructor(s), students, content, pedagogy, and context. Consequently, sweeping generalizations about how to implement or assess a learning community that are not context bound may be counterproductive because they do not account for differences in students, instructors, or context. Although Meiklejohn and Dewey are helpful guides in understanding the history of learning communities, their contribution is anachronistic because it does not address the existence of a learning community in the context of today's complex postsecondary institution. New conceptual models are needed to guide the implementation and assessment of learning communities. In their comprehensive review of research related to college impact, Pascarella and Terenzini (2005) encouraged researchers and administrators to acknowledge the multitude of factors affecting student change, and to adopt broader conceptual models that might "more fully account for the multiple sources of influence," (p. 630) instead of relying upon a single disciplinary perspective or dimension of students' experiences.

Several human ecology researchers include the social contexts in which development occurs, which is helpful when conceptualizing or assessing learning communities. Influenced by Kurt Lewin's (1936) proposition that behavior is a function of a person and an environment, two complementary human ecology models developed virtually simultaneously. The ecology of human development, which arose from Urie Bronfenbrenner's (1979) work exploring infant and adolescent development, was one model, and Rudolph Moos's (1979) social ecology model, which examined the impact of the physical and social environment on human beings, was another model.

Bronfenbrenner's Ecological Systems Theory. Bronfenbrenner (1979) emphasized the importance of studying human development in the context of "the actual environments, both immediate and remote, in which human beings live" (p. 12). His theory stressed the importance of considering development within the context it occurs, and specifically how biological factors—including physical characteristics and genetic propensities—interact with the "immediate environment, *and* the way in which this relation is mediated by forces emanating from more remote regions in the larger physical and social milieu" (Bronfenbrenner, 1979, pp. 12–13, italics in the original). Renn and Arnold (2003) encouraged researchers and administrators to consider Bronfenbrenner's model to gain a more holistic understanding of the learning environment, including the influence of peer culture. When considering the effectiveness of a learning community, the theory focuses one's gaze on students' experiences and the myriad environments that may shape their experiences, including formal and informal social and academic interactions, the broader university environment, and larger social structures affecting the student. Bronfenbrenner's model illustrates how personal attributes, called developmentally instigative characteristics, set in motion "reciprocal processes of interpersonal interaction" (p. 12) that affect learning. He outlined four types of these characteristics, including *personal stimulus characteristics*, *selective responsivity*, *structuring proclivities*, and *directive beliefs*. Perhaps most relevant to conceptualizing a learning community environment is Bronfenbrenner's (1993) first type, *personal stimulus characteristics*, which details how people's actions invite or inhibit particular responses from the environment that can disrupt or foster psychological growth (e.g., how peers might respond differently to a shy versus outgoing member of their learning community). Bronfenbrenner's second type, *selective responsivity*, describes how people interact with their surroundings (e.g., some students may immerse themselves fully in the learning community, attending activities outside of class and contributing regularly to discussion, while others might treat their learning community experience as they would any other class). The third type, *structuring proclivities*, details how people seek out increasingly complex activities (e.g., students may wrestle with disciplinary differences and ultimately integrate and cohere knowledge from two related courses). The fourth type, *directive beliefs*, refers to how people view their agency in relation to their environment (e.g., students who have a deep disciplinary grounding may feel more or less able to engage actively in the content of another discipline).

In a learning community, students possessing varying developmentally instigative characteristics interact with one another in addition to interacting with the faculty and student affairs administrators who are affiliated with the community. These interactions shape students' academic and social integration and ultimately affect their learning.

Another important aspect of Bronfenbrenner's (1993) model is the context, described as the environmental characteristics that interact with the person and affect developmental processes. Bronfenbrenner envisioned these characteristics as nested systems that surround an individual, from proximal to distal. He labeled these the micro-, meso-, exo-, and macrosystem.

Most relevant to understanding students' experiences in learning communities are microsystems because they include the student and learning community context. The microsystem is defined by Bronfenbrenner (1993) as "a pattern of activities, roles, and interpersonal relations" that are experienced in one's immediate environment that "invite, permit, or inhibit engagement" in that environment (p. 15). Within a learning community, there are aspects of students' microsystems that are identical, including their paired courses and cocurricular activities.

The mesosystem, defined as "a system of two or more settings frequented by the same person" (Bronfenbrenner, 1993, p. 20), details the linkages students may make to their shared microsystems (learning community), which may include their home, family, or peer group. While other elements of the context (exo- and macrosystems) may affect students' developmental processes and experiences, they are more distal and do not contain the student.

Bronfenbrenner's model adds complexity to the way in which administrators and researchers conceptualize a learning community, encouraging them to consider not only what students bring to the community and their experiences within the community, but also the other factors that influence students' experiences, from financial aid policies to the ease of pairing courses through the registrar's office.

Moos's Social–Ecological Framework. Simultaneous to the emergence of the ecology of human development, social ecology, "the multidisciplinary study of the impact that physical and social environments have on human beings" (Moos & Insel, 1974, pp. ix–x), arose out of Stanford

University. Whereas the ecology of human development emphasized the interaction of direct and indirect environmental effects on biologically determined development (Bronfenbrenner, 1979), social ecology theory placed more emphasis on the immediate physical environment as a mediator of development, and underscored the importance of creating a physical and psychological environment that promotes effective human functioning (Moos & Insel, 1974). Consequently, Moos's work might be particularly useful when conceptualizing or assessing living-learning community environments because of their physical dimension.

Moos's (1979) model "notes the existence of both environmental and personal systems, which influence each other through selection factors . . . [and] mediating processes of cognitive appraisal and activation or arousal (motivation)" (p. 4). These mediation processes typically arise when the environment necessitates a response and result in efforts at adaptation and use of coping skills. The initiation of adaptation efforts may change both the environmental and the personal systems, and ultimately determines stability or change in student behavior.

The Environmental System. Moos (1979) described four major domains of variables within the environmental system, including "the physical setting, organizational factors, human aggregate, and social climate" (p. 6), each of which can potentially influence educational outcomes directly or indirectly through interaction with the other environmental variables. The physical setting includes the physical design and architecture of the environment. In a residential learning community, the physical setting may include the building in which the community is housed, the presence or lack of study and gathering spaces, and the amenities provided. Organizational factors include such dimensions as size of the learning community, paired classes, and offerings provided to students in the way of cocurricular activities. The human aggregate is composed of the total characteristics of students in the setting, and may include "age, ability level, socioeconomic background, and educational attainment" (p. 8). Faculty and staff characteristics may also be part of the human aggregate. Moos found the human aggregate pertinent to the environmental system because of the "notion that most of the social and cultural environment is transmitted through other people," and the implication that "the character of an environment depends in part on the typical characteristics of its members" (p. 8). Also included in the human aggregate would be the collective attitudes of students and their collective beliefs about the environment as promoting or thwarting their educational pursuits. The fourth domain, social climate, is inferred by the "continuity and consistency in otherwise discrete events" (p. 10). Within a learning community, the social climate would be the integrating features of the environment, including the students' overall attitudes toward each other and their beliefs about the role of peers in their learning. In addition to serving as a domain of the environmental setting, Moos viewed the social climate as a mediator of the other environmental variables.

The Personal System. As might be expected, individual characteristics that assist in explaining students' responses to an environmental context comprise the personal system. "Background and personal indexes include age, sex, ability level, interests and values, ego strength and self-esteem, and preferences for such coping styles as active engagement in the environment, tension reduction and exploration" (Moos, 1979, p. 11). Other personal factors considered within the personal system include attitudes, expectations, and roles. Moos explained that "People who have more responsible organizational roles (such as administrators, professors, and teachers, as compared with high school and college students) tend to perceive educational settings more positively," and furthermore, "Expectations of new environments can influence both an individual's choice and later perception of an environment" (p. 11).

Mediating Factors. Moos (1979) identified two factors that mediate the interaction between the environmental system and the personal system, namely, (a) *cognitive appraisal* and (b) *activation or arousal.* Cognitive appraisal is the process by which an individual evaluates the environment as "being either potentially harmful, beneficial, or irrelevant (primary appraisal) and his or her perception of the range of available coping alternatives (secondary appraisal)" (p. 11). Activation or arousal occurs when an individual appraises the environment as needing a response, which in turn "prompts efforts at adaptation, or coping, which may change the environmental system (students decide to use a recreation room as a library or study hall) or the personal system (students seek and obtain information that changes their attitudes or expectations)" (p. 12).

Coping and Adaptation. Moos (1979) explained that although situations chosen to study coping and adaptation usually involve major life changes including death, financial disaster, and serious illness, more common transitions and everyday situations also demand coping responses. Learning community outcomes, such as students' transition to college, persistence, development of cognitive complexity, and social and academic integration could be assessed through Moos's model because they illustrate how students cope with and adapt to their environment. Like Bronfenbrenner's (1979) model, Moos's model encourages administrators and researchers to consider a variety of factors when designing and assessing learning communities. Unique to Moos's model is the emphasis on the physical environment, which is not often considered in learning community research and assessment and may help to unpack some of the tacit cultural messages that students within the community receive.

Conclusion

Having evolved from an innovation adopted to improve the quality of higher education, learning communities are now an integral part of many postsecondary institutions (Matthews et al., 2012). As these communities become more commonplace, it is important not to lose sight of the theoretical underpinnings that guided their initial structure and function and the research that directs best practices in their implementation. In addition, as postsecondary institutions continue to increase in complexity, it is vital that administrators and scholars adopt more multifaceted models for conceptualizing and assessing these communities, acknowledging the myriad issues that affect their structure and the students within them.

References

Association of American Colleges. (1985). *Integrity in the curriculum: A report to the academic community*. Washington, DC: Author.

Association of American Colleges and Universities (AAC&U). (2002). *Greater expectations: A new vision for learning as a nation goes to college*. Washington, DC: Author.

Association of American Colleges and Universities (AAC&U). (2007). *College learning and the new global century*. Washington, DC: Author.

Astin, A. W. (1984). Student involvement: A developmental theory for higher education. *Journal of College Student Development*, *25*, 297–308.

Boyer Commission on Educating Undergraduates in the Research University. (1998). *Reinventing undergraduate education: A blueprint for America's research universities*. Stony Brook: State University of New York at Stony Brook.

Bronfenbrenner, U. (1979). *The ecology of human development: Experiments by nature and design*. Cambridge, MA: Harvard University.

Bronfenbrenner, U. (1993). The ecology of cognitive development: Research models and fugitive findings. In R. H. Wozniak & K. W. Fischer (Eds.), *Development in context: Acting and thinking in specific environments* (pp. 3–44). Hillsdale, NJ: Erlbaum.

Cox, B. E., & Orehovec, E. (2007). Faculty-student interaction outside the classroom: A typology from a residential college. *The Review of Higher Education*, *30*, 343–362.

Dewey, J. (1916). *Democracy and education*. New York, NY: Macmillan.

Dewey, J. (1938). *Experience and education*. New York, NY: Collier.

Dewey, J. (1974). The child and the curriculum. In R. D. Archambault (Ed.), *John Dewey on education: Selected writings* (pp. 339–358). Chicago, IL: University of Chicago.

Gabelnick, F., MacGregor, J., Matthews, R. S., & Smith, B. L. (Eds.). (1990). *New Directions for Teaching and Learning: No. 41. Learning communities: Creating connections among students, faculty, and disciplines*. San Francisco, CA: Jossey-Bass.

Garrison, D. R., & Anderson, T. (2003). *E-learning in the 21st century: A framework for research and practice*. New York, NY: Routledge.

Garrison, D. R., Anderson, T., & Archer, W. (2000). Critical inquiry in a text-based environment: Computer conferencing in higher education. *The Internet and Higher Education*, 2, 87–105.

Golde, C. M., & Pribbenow, D. A. (2000). Understanding faculty involvement in residential learning communities. *Journal of College Student Development*, *41*(1), 27–40.

Klein, J. T., & Newell, W. H. (1997). Advancing interdisciplinary studies. In J. G. Gaff, J. L. Ratcliff, & Associates (Eds.), *Handbook of the undergraduate curriculum* (pp. 393–415). Washington, DC: Association of American Colleges & Universities.

Kuh, G. D. (2008). *High-impact educational practices: What they are, who has access to them, and why they matter*. Washington, DC: Association of American Colleges and Universities.

Lenning, O. T., & Ebbers, L. H. (1999). *The powerful potential of learning communities: Improving education for the future* (ASHE-ERIC Higher Education Reports, 26[6]). Washington, DC: Graduate School of Education and Human Development, The George Washington University.

Lenning, O. T., Hill, D. M., Saunders, K. P., Solan, A., & Stokes, A. (2013). *Powerful learning communities: A guide to developing student, faculty and professional learning communities to improve student success and organizational effectiveness*. Sterling, VA: Stylus.

Lewin, K. (1936). *Principles of topological psychology*. New York, NY: McGraw-Hill.

Lichtenstein, M. (2005). The importance of classroom environments in the assessment of learning community outcomes. *Journal of College Student Development*, *46*(4), 341–356.

Matthews, R. S., Smith, B. L., & MacGregor, J. (2012). The evolution of learning communities: A retrospective. In K. Buch & K. E. Barron (Eds.), *New Directions for Teaching and Learning: No. 132. Discipline centered learning communities* (pp. 99–111). San Francisco, CA: Jossey-Bass.

Matthews, R. S., Smith, B. L., MacGregor, J., & Gabelnick, F. (1997). Creating learning communities. In J. G. Gaff, J. L. Ratcliff, & Associates (Eds.), *Handbook of the undergraduate curriculum* (pp. 457–475). Washington, DC: Association of American Colleges and Universities.

Moos, R. H. (1979). *Evaluating educational environments*. San Francisco, CA: Jossey-Bass.

Moos, R. H., & Insel, P. M. (1974). *Issues in social ecology: Human milieus*. Palo Alto, CA: National Press Books.

Palloff, R. M., & Pratt, K. (2007). *Building online learning communities: Effective strategies for the online classroom* (2nd ed.). San Francisco, CA: Jossey-Bass.

Pascarella, E. T., & Terenzini, P. T. (2005). *How college affects students*. San Francisco, CA: Jossey-Bass.

Renn, K. A., & Arnold, K. D. (2003). Reconceptualizing research on college student peer culture. *Journal of Higher Education*, *74*, 261–291.

Shapiro, N. S., & Levine, J. H. (1999). *Creating learning communities: A practical guide to winning support, organizing for change, and implementing programs*. San Francisco, CA: Jossey-Bass.

Taylor, K., Moore, W. S., MacGregor, J., & Lindblad, J. (2003). *What we know now about learning community research and assessment* [National Learning Communities Project monograph series]. Olympia, WA: Washington Center for Improving the Quality of Undergraduate Education, The Evergreen State College.

Tinto, V. (1993). *Leaving college: Rethinking the causes and cures of student attrition* (2nd ed.). Chicago, IL: University of Chicago.

Tinto, V., Goodsell Love, A., & Russo, P. (1994). *Building learning communities for new college students: A summary of research findings of the collaborative learning project*. University Park, PA: The Pennsylvania State University, National Center for Teaching, Learning, and Assessment.

Wawrzynski, M. R., & Jessup-Anger, J. E. (2010). From expectations to experiences: Using a structural typology to understand first-year student outcomes in academically based living-learning environments. *Journal of College Student Development*, *51*(2), 201–217.

Wawrzynski, M. R., Jessup-Anger, J. E., Helman, C., Stolz, K., & Beaulieu, J. (2009). Exploring students' perceptions of academically based living-learning communities. *College Student Affairs Journal*, *28*, 138–158.

Wingspread Group on Higher Education. (1993). *American imperative: Higher expectations for higher education*. Racine, WI: The Johnson Foundation.

JODY E. JESSUP-ANGER is an assistant professor of higher education in the Department of Educational Policy and Leadership Studies at Marquette University.

3

This chapter explores the practices of learning communities designed for specific, underserved student populations, highlighting on-campus examples and culminating with a synthesized list of core practices from these "inclusive" learning communities.

With Educational Benefits for All: Campus Inclusion Through Learning Communities Designed for Underserved Student Populations

John E. Fink, Mary L. Hummel

High-impact educational practices, such as learning communities, service learning, and study abroad, create "seamless learning environments" wherein students connect learning across multiple contexts (e.g., lecture, dining halls, internships), fostering engaged learning experiences for participants. Scholars identified a variety of educational benefits associated with participation in these high-impact practices (Kuh, 2008). Yet, other scholars questioned whether higher education institutions have adequately engaged underserved students, such as students of color, first-generation students, and transfer students, in these high-impact educational practices (Engstrom & Tinto, 1998). As Harper and Quaye (2009) claimed in their sourcebook for engaging diverse populations in higher education, not intentionally designing educational practices to serve the plurality of learners on contemporary college campuses equates to institutional negligence in sharing responsibility for all students' success. Among these high-impact practices, learning communities have a legacy of undergraduate educational reform and are cultivating a contemporary role of serving underrepresented students in higher education (Engstrom & Tinto, 2008; Lardner, 2003).

An "Equity-Minded" Approach to Learning Communities

Learning communities designed for underserved student populations are emerging, and by nature of their target populations these programs are well positioned to assist institutions in delivering quality educational experiences to traditionally underserved students. The American Association of Colleges and Universities (AAC&U) is leading efforts to examine and

Published online in Wiley Online Library (wileyonlinelibrary.com) • DOI: 10.1002/ss.20115

address inequity among high-impact practices, such as learning communities. *Assessing Underserved Students' Engagement in High-Impact Practices* (Finley & McNair, 2013) presents findings from a mixed-methods study adding to the evidence that high-impact practices yield a variety of positive college outcomes, particularly for underserved students. These authors concluded with a call to campus administrators to enhance student success through expanding participation in high-impact practices to the entire student population. In AAC&U's related Making Excellence Inclusive (MEI) initiative, scholars applied the concept of equity mindedness, which asserts that institutional practices, not student deficits, are responsible for the educational success of all students (Bensimon, 2007). Our approach to suggesting "core practices" of learning communities in this chapter applies the concept of equity mindedness in order to amplify learning community efforts that ultimately make excellence inclusive by supporting the success of underserved student populations. We will refer to these as *inclusive* learning communities, intentionally designed and implemented to benefit traditionally underserved students.

There are numerous underserved populations in higher education including students with disabilities, international students, LGBT-identified students, returning students, and student veterans (Harper & Quaye, 2009). A full review of each underserved student population in higher education was beyond the scope of this chapter. Thus, our description of core practices of these inclusive learning communities focuses on existing programs designed to serve students of color, first-generation and low-income students, transfer students, and women in science and engineering. We selected these student populations because learning communities have been successfully developed and may be used as models for others. While students in these diverse populations have unique needs that must be taken into account when creating and sustaining individual learning community programs, we find that a common theme across these inclusive learning communities is their potential to bridge institutional goals to both enhance educational quality and promote student success.

Relevant Literature on Inclusive Learning Community Practices

As learning communities have proliferated, numerous books and articles have described effective learning communities and core practices, and these suggestions lend insight to the ideal practices of inclusive learning communities. Smith, MacGregor, Matthews, and Gabelnick's (2004) book was a landmark work that built on previous scholarship (e.g., Lenning & Ebbers, 1999; Shapiro & Levine, 1999) suggesting five core practices of learning communities: community, diversity, integration, active learning, and reflection/assessment. Smith et al. (2004) described these five core practices as overlapping areas, and the authors provided a list of suggested practices including fostering students' sense of connectedness both socially and academically to the university community, affirming diversity in learning styles through implementing inclusive pedagogy, and engaging students to be active learners and make connections across disciplines.

More recently, Lenning, Hill, Saunders, Solan, and Stokes (2013) aimed to create a comprehensive guide for learning community practitioners in their book *Powerful Learning Communities: A Guide to Developing Students, Faculty, and Professional Learning Communities to Improve Student Success and Organizational Effectiveness*. Partially informed by a survey of learning communities at 81 institutions, the authors offered 25 "essential processes" for planning, implementing, and sustaining learning communities. Yet, these authors offered scant suggestions specific to learning communities that focus on underserved student populations. While much learning community practitioner scholarship exists, in addition to substantial works on serving diverse student populations such as Harper and Quaye's (2009) *Student Engagement in Higher Education*, scholarship on learning communities specifically designed to support underserved students in higher education is only emerging.

In a case study, Jehangir (2009) presented the "Multicultural Learning Community" (MLC) and characterized the impact of learning community participation on a cohort of low-income, first-generation students at a large research university in the Midwest. Students in this cohort enrolled in three linked courses in which they connected across disciplines around themes of identity, community, and social agency. Examining qualitative data from reflective writing assignments, Jehangir derived several themes characterizing how students experienced the MLC. One set of themes connected students' sense of belonging to the community and strong bond among cohort members to the practice of critical pedagogy, wherein students were invited to cocreate knowledge in the classroom setting by sharing their identity and personal experiences. Jehangir found that students developed a capacity for self-authorship, arguing that the MLC provided a supportive, affirming space for students to find their voice. In this case study, Jehangir also described these first-generation college students as being able to "build bridges" between the higher education setting and their contexts outside the university.

Chávez's (2007) study similarly explored core practices of multicultural learning communities, yet focused on the characteristics of four faculty members nominated by students as multiculturally empowering leaders. Students commented that these faculty members created safe and supportive learning community environments by taking class time to set explicit ground rules for dialogue, such as speaking from experience, listening, acknowledging differences, and challenging ideas and assumptions. Chávez characterized this "climate of safety" as appreciative of difference, inclusive of all students, yet also balanced with a "spirit of risk taking," noting that "safety within an empowered learning collective does not mean a lack of discomfort" (p. 280).

Chávez (2007) and Jehangir (2009) contributed to the learning community practitioner literature by describing effective multicultural teaching practices within learning communities designed for underserved students. Building on the work of these authors, as well as literature on underserved student populations (e.g., Harper & Quaye, 2009) and learning community practitioners (e.g., Lenning et al., 2013), the next section synthesizes core practices of learning communities designed for underserved student populations, illustrated by specific program examples from a range of colleges and universities.

Core Practices of Inclusive Learning Communities

Common practices emerged as we explored scholarship and practice related to how learning communities supported underserved student populations. Using these core characteristics, we developed a framework for consideration that can be generalized across program and institutional types. Specific learning community examples illustrate the following core practices of inclusive learning communities, designed with focus on a particular underserved student population: using population-specific theory and research to inform practice; fostering students' bond to each other and sense of belonging to the institution; engaging students as active learners in the campus community; creating a positive message of achievement and change; and advocating on behalf of the student constituency toward systemic improvement throughout the institution.

Using Population-Specific Theory and Research to Inform Practice. Using relevant theory and research to inform programs, structure, and curriculum is critical to creating an effective, population-specific learning community. Such scholarship can help practitioners better understand the experience of underserved students in higher education, including the aspects of the college environment that are most challenging and most supportive. This recommendation is consistent with Lenning et al.'s (2013) claim that powerful learning communities regularly use research and assessment data to drive processes of continual improvement. Yet, with a targeted focus on a particular student population, learning communities for underserved students can draw on relevant, population-specific literature bases in addition to program-level assessment. For example, *Student Engagement in Higher Education*, edited by Shaun R. Harper and Stephen J. Quaye (2009), presented strategies for intentionally designing educational practices to engage a variety of underserved student populations, informed by relevant, population-specific theory and research. Considering the scholarship specific to a learning community's student constituency is absolutely critical to creating and sustaining a successful program. For example, Hawkins and Larabee (2009) argued that students of color at predominately White institutions (PWIs) "choose not to become involved in learning communities because they often lack culturally appealing activities" (p. 183). In their recommendations for engaging racial and ethnic minorities in their first year at PWIs, Hawkins and Larabee suggested that learning community practitioners "incorporate relevant cultural and historical themes" (p. 194), informed in part by focus groups of the intended student population. Furthermore, learning community practitioners may also use population-specific information from theory, research, and program assessment to carry out another of Lenning et al.'s (2013) "essential processes": clearly defining program goals and outcomes for learning community stakeholders.

The Transfer2Terp (T2T) Learning Community at the University of Maryland exemplifies the core practice of using population-specific theory and research to inform practice (J. Fink, personal communication, August 13, 2013). Designed to mitigate challenges that transfer students encountered transitioning from community college to a large research university, practitioners relied on national and campus-specific research on transfer students to create program goals and components. Grounded in scholarship calling for more intentional integration of transfer students into the social and academic fabric of research universities (for example, Townsend & Wilson, 2006), as well as inequities in rates of participation in "high-impact practices" among community college transfer students (for example, Ishitani & McKitrick, 2010), developers of the T2T program selected three program goals: (a) to assist students with the transition to the life and culture of a research institution; (b) to engage students in leadership, identity, and civic development involvement opportunities; and (c) to encourage a sense of belonging and interconnectedness with the campus community.

The program engages students in a seminar course aimed at equipping students for academic success, while also leveraging the resources of its coordinating unit, the Stamp Student Union and Center for Campus Life, to connect students to enriching cocurricular involvement opportunities. Even the name "Transfer2Terp" symbolically represents the program's grounding in Schlossberg's (1984) transition theory, which practitioners use to communicate the program's mission to ease students' "moving in, moving through, moving out" transition process as they simultaneously transition from "transfers" to "Terps" (the university's mascot).

Fostering Students' Bond to Each Other and Sense of Belonging to the Institution. Another core practice of learning communities designed for underserved student populations is fostering relationships among students and creating a sense of belonging to the institution. Smith et al. (2004) described this core practice as creating a community of inclusion, and Lenning et al. (2013) added that powerful learning communities are created with both emotional and intellectual bonds among members. Learning communities designed for underserved student populations are especially important in fostering a sense of belonging among members as they often are supplementing some degree of unmet needs for their specific student population. For example, students of color at PWIs often experience isolation, a need to prove themselves, or pressure to be the sole voice on behalf of their racial identity, directly affecting their ability to feel as if they belong to the campus community (Quaye, Tambascia, & Talesh, 2009). In fact, the benefits of fostering students' bond to each other and sense of belonging have contributed to students' increased self-confidence, as well as feelings of validation as members of the university community (Engstrom & Tinto, 2008). Additionally, findings from Chávez (2007) and Jehangir (2009) supported the notion that safe and supportive environments are critical to the success of learning communities. Students in these learning communities experienced class climates that were supportive, appreciative of difference, conscious of inclusivity and class participation, as well as focused on learning and growth of the students and faculty. Furthermore, Lenning et al. (2013) echoed both Chávez (2007) and Jehangir (2009) in suggesting that while learning communities must create supportive environments, they must also create space for conflicting opinions to be resolved respectfully and constructively in order to advance each member's learning.

One example of facilitating this connection is by connecting underserved students to role models and mentors who not only provide a personal illustration of success but also share some common experiences or identities with their mentees. Some students from these underserved populations may enter postsecondary education without familial role models or examples of higher education achievement from their precollege experiences. Learning communities have a great potential to provide role models in a meaningful way to connect students to others in a desired professional field.

Exemplifying the core practice of fostering students' bond to each other and a sense of belonging, the Women in Science and Engineering (WISE) program began in 1995 at the University of Wisconsin–Madison to develop community, leadership skills, and a sense of belonging for women enrolled in science, technology, engineering, and mathematics (STEM) fields in which they were traditionally underrepresented. Women in the program live with 75 other first-year women science and engineering majors on a residence hall floor in a specific building. They participate in mentoring as well as social and career activities through the year. In addition, students can take a WISE section of fundamental math/science courses.

One of the key aspects of the program is the mentoring/role model function that occurs. Being able to talk with other women students, as well as staff and faculty at various stages in their careers, is essential to helping students succeed. It has the added benefit of providing a key leadership opportunity to sophomore women as they develop leadership skills through their role as peer mentors. Through the course work, the WISE activities, peer mentors, and networking, the program is designed to enhance achievement and retention of women in the pipeline for these academic disciplines. Assessment of this success is evidenced by the data that regardless of grade-point average, participation in WISE is associated with a 140% increase in STEM graduation rate for women (Meiller, 2012).

The WISE program at the University of Wisconsin–Madison is but one example of similar programs across the country designed to support women enrolled in STEM majors. In 1993, the University of Michigan established a WISE program where students lived in a coed residence hall, but on a specific floor designated for the program participants. In addition to enrolling in specific math/chemistry courses together, they had a variety of programming events and opportunities to connect with faculty and professional mentors. Other WISE programs exist at a variety of institutions such as Iowa State University, the University of Iowa, and Clemson University. This proliferation of programs is indicative of the mentoring need.

Engaging Students as Active Learners in the Campus Community. Learning communities constructed as interventions to improve the retention of underserved populations are commonplace in higher education. However, to realize the full potential of the learning communities, active learning must be a core practice. This recommendation is of particular importance for learning communities designed for underserved student populations. Historically, higher education institutions have not adequately provided equitable access to enriching educational opportunities wherein students would engage as active learners in the campus community. By designing and implementing learning communities specifically focused on underserved student populations, institutions are better positioned to equitably distribute the educational benefits of active learning to all students.

Two examples illustrate how a learning community designed for underserved students can engage students as active learners in the campus community. Created in 1989, the Undergraduate Research Opportunity Program (UROP) at the University of Michigan (Hummel, 2008) was designed to increase achievement and retention of underrepresented students by connecting them to the academic mission of the research university. The program, open to all students, provides a hands-on learning experience for first- and second-year students through research partnerships with faculty in all academic disciplines. Students develop research and academic skills through experiential work and mentoring experiences with faculty and graduate student research teams. In addition, students have a peer mentor who leads the research seminar where they discuss their projects and experiences and learn about the resources of the university. By participating in research from the start at the university, students discover new competencies, strengthen their intellectual curiosity, and clarify their academic and professional goals.

More recently, the TransferUnited (TU) living-learning program was created at the University of North Carolina (UNC), Chapel Hill, to address lower graduation and retention rates of junior transfers from community colleges (A. Fisher, personal communication, August 21, 2013). While the program has the goals of connecting students to campus life as well as promoting student wellness, a major focus of TU is to introduce students to the rigor and academic mission of UNC-Chapel Hill. In their learning community seminar course, students engage in a semester-long autoethnography research project examining their transition into the Chapel Hill community and requiring them to conduct two hours of fieldwork each week, interviewing and observing members of the campus community. Concurrent with the seminar is an "academic success group" that runs the first eight weeks of the semester and focuses on teaching students about campus resources and academic success skills. The TU learning community exemplifies how learning communities can engage underserved transfer students as active learners in the campus community.

Creating a Positive Message of Achievement and Change. In addition to providing opportunities for active learning in connection to the academic mission, the message given to underserved students is critical. When learning communities are created in response to an institutional problem, such as lower retention or graduation rates, keeping the focus on institutional solutions and positive individual messages is essential. Effective learning communities that focus on underserved student populations will leverage positive messages of achievement and change to yield desired outcomes. Practitioners working with underserved student populations must be mindful of avoiding deficit-focused framing of programs, services, and goals, remembering that the "problem" exists on the institutional level and not on the individual student level. Rather, practitioners who frame the learning community as enhancing students' college experiences through a series of program offerings, such as research opportunities, faculty mentorship, or linked courses, will be better positioned to support underserved student populations. Furthermore, as Engstrom and Tinto (2008) concluded, learning community practitioners ideally will both set high expectations and provide high levels of support, and their caring attitude can contribute to students' confidence in themselves and their achievement.

One of the long-standing models that illustrates this positive message of achievement is the Building Educational Strengths and Talents (BEST) program, which presents an example of creating a positive message of achievement and change (T. Lucas, personal communication, August 16, 2013). Established in 1988 at the University of North Carolina at Charlotte (UNCC), BEST was created to improve academic performance, increase retention and graduation rates, and minimize "time-to-degree." BEST was primarily created to serve first-generation college students but is also open to students with limited financial ability and/or with a learning disability. The 164 participants, described as "Achievers," have access to tutors, instruction in basic study skills, access to state-of-the-art technology, assistance in communication skills, and support for graduate school admission/financial processes. One of the initial activities is a dinner that staff members serve to the students and their family members to help with the transition period and allow students to begin to see their often two very different worlds interact. In their seminar, one of the first assignments is to write an intergenerational paper titled "I stand on your shoulders" discussing their values in the context of UNCC expectations. Through these activities, these

"Achievers" create and benefit from a positive message of educational attainment and change.

One of the challenges in implementing this practice is how to recruit students into these learning communities with a positive message, rather than framing student participants as deficient in some way. The T2T Learning Community provides one example of how to create this positive message of achievement and change in the recruitment process. T2T practitioners start with the understanding that the transfer students they are recruiting have already demonstrated success at their community college. Therefore, the program focuses on offering students support in translating their success at community college to the new campus environment. Furthermore, T2T utilizes a strengths-based curriculum rooted in positive psychology, which guides students through the development of their talents into strengths and application of those strengths to academic success. In sum, the T2T learning community affirms students' previous accomplishments and offers support as students continue to build on their past successes toward future achievement.

Advocating on Behalf of the Student Constituency Toward Systemic Improvement Throughout the Institution. Part of the framing of positive individual achievement is a focus on how to address institutional structures not designed to meet varying student needs. Learning communities designed for underserved students are most effective when they also advocate for systemic improvement across campus for the entire underserved population. It is uncommon that a learning community designed for underserved students will be able to enroll all members from that particular campus population. Thus, practitioners who focus on improving institution-wide barriers and challenges encountered by the specific student population served by their learning community directly benefit not only their students but the broader campus population as well. Furthermore, Lenning et al. (2013) argued that powerful learning communities contribute to institutions' core missions, get buy-in from and work collaboratively with key campus partners, and employ institutional change frameworks to advance their efforts on campus. Learning communities focused on underserved populations can build on the advice from Lenning et al. to the benefit of a particular student population across campus. These learning community practitioners, often seen as campus experts on the particular student population, can use the learning community as a powerful catalyst of institutional change to improve, align, or create services for the benefit of the entire underserved student population.

Two campus examples illustrate the work of learning community practitioners as advocates for underserved student populations. Responding to a Pell study (Engle & Tinto, 2008) that showed only 11% of first-generation college students completed college in six years, the University of Cincinnati created the Gen 1 program in 2008 (Fuller, 2008). Practitioners identified that these first-generation students were less likely to live on campus due to financial barriers. Thus, one aspect of the program was the development of a model that provides financial support to help subsidize the cost of campus housing. In addition, Gen 1 staff worked with a variety of other units on campus including admissions, financial aid, the learning assistance center, and the library to align services to meet the unique needs of this student cohort. The Gen 1 program approached advocacy and the removal of barriers in several ways. Not only was there a practical, financial aspect, but also they made others on campus aware of a population of students not obviously visible but with important, unmet needs (C. Black, personal communication, August 12, 2013).

Additionally, the T2T Learning Community focused primarily in its pilot year on partnering with campus units to enhance the experience among program participants, yet T2T also catalyzed campus-wide advocacy on behalf of community college transfer students. Responding directly to student concerns with their transfer orientation program, practitioners partnered with the orientation office to win a campus grant supporting an enhancement of the orientation program for all transfer students. Additionally, student members of T2T, conscious of the substantially larger transfer student population compared to the size of the learning community, created a support group open to all transfer students and worked with practitioners to outreach to their community college to share insight around the transfer process with prospective students. In T2T's second year, program staff capitalized on excitement from a successful first year, initiating a campus-wide "Transfer Experience Network" to align existing services among academic affairs and student affairs staff working directly with transfer students. Offering expertise on the student population, as well as a focus group of students to direct advocacy efforts, learning communities designed for underserved student populations can catalyze improvement of campus programs and services.

Conclusion

From our examination of learning communities designed for underserved student populations, we suggest five core practices of these "inclusive" learning communities. Key to success is utilizing theory and research concerning specific target populations in order to address specific issues and barriers. Creating a significant bond among members of the community and to the institution as a whole provides a supportive environment in which to grow, develop, and succeed. Positive messages of achievement and success are also important in helping students achieve academically and graduate. Finally, a focus not only on individual concerns but also on how the institutional systems can be changed to improve for all students is essential. Through these principles, learning communities can create opportunities for underserved students to participate fully in the educational environment, thereby making excellence inclusive.

References

Bensimon, E. M. (2007). The underestimated significance of practitioner knowledge in the scholarship on student success. *Review of Higher Education, 30*(4), 441–469.

Chávez, A. F. (2007). Islands of empowerment: Facilitating multicultural learning communities in college. *International Journal of Teaching and Learning in Higher Education, 19*(3), 274–288.

Engle, J., & Tinto, V. (2008). *Moving beyond access: College success for low-income, first generation students*. Washington, DC: The Pell Institute for the Study of Opportunity in Higher Education.

Engstrom, C., & Tinto, V. (1998). Access without support is not opportunity. *Change, 40*(1), 46–50.

Engstrom, C., & Tinto, V. (2008). Learning better together: The impact of learning communities on the persistence of low-income students. *Opportunity Matters, 1*, 5–21.

Finley, A., & McNair, T. (2013). *Assessing underserved students' engagement in high-impact practices*. Washington, DC: Association of American Colleges and Universities.

Fuller, D. (2008, September). UC introduces new living and learning community for first generation college students. *UC News—UC Magazine*. Retrieved from http://www.uc.edu/News/NR.aspx?ID=8811

Harper, S. R., & Quaye, S. J. (2009). Beyond sameness, with engagement and outcomes for all. In S. R. Harper & S. J. Quaye (Eds.), *Student engagement in higher education* (pp. 1–15). New York, NY: Routledge.

Hawkins, V. M., & Larabee, H. J. (2009). Engaging racial/ethnic minority students in out-of-class activities on predominantly white campuses. In S. R. Harper & S. J. Quaye (Eds.), *Student engagement in higher education* (pp. 179–197). New York, NY: Routledge.

Hummel, M. L. (2008). Social justice as a strategy for residence hall community development. In W. Zeller (Ed.), *Residence life programs and the new student experience* (pp. 67–74). Columbia, SC: ACUHO-I and the National Resource Center for the First Year Experience and Students in Transition.

Ishitani, T. T., & McKitrick, S. A. (2010). After transfer: The engagement of community college students at a four-year collegiate institution. *Community College Journal of Research and Practice, 34*, 576–594.

Jehangir, R. (2009). Cultivating voice: First-generation students seek full academic citizenship in multicultural learning communities. *Innovative Higher Education, 34*(1), 33–49.

Kuh, G. D. (2008). *High-impact educational practices: What they are, who has access to them, and why they matter*. Washington, DC: Association of American Colleges and Universities.

Lardner, E. D. (2003). *Approaching diversity through learning communities*. Olympia, WA: The Evergreen State College, Washington Center for Improving the Quality of Undergraduate Education.

Lenning, O. T., & Ebbers, L. H. (1999). *The powerful potential of learning communities: Improving education for the future* (ASHE-ERIC Higher Education Report, 26[6]). Washington DC: Graduate School of Education and Human Development, The George Washington University.

Lenning, O. T., Hill, D. M., Saunders, K. P., Solan, A., & Stokes, A. (2013). *Powerful learning communities: A guide to developing student, faculty, and professional learning communities to improve student success and organizational effectiveness*. Sterling, VA: Stylus.

Meiller, R. (2012). Residential community helps science-minded college women succeed. *Wisconsin News-Online University News*. Retrieved from http://www.news.wisc.edu/20461

Quaye, S. J., Tambascia, T. P., & Talesh, R. A. (2009). Engaging racial/ethnic minority students in predominantly white classroom environments. In S. R. Harper & S. J. Quaye (Eds.), *Student engagement in higher education* (pp. 57–78). New York, NY: Routledge.

Schlossberg, N. K. (1984). *Counseling adults in transition: Linking practice with theory*. New York, NY: Springer.

Shapiro, N. S., & Levine, J. H. (1999). *Creating learning communities: A practical guide to winning support, organizing for change, and implementing programs*. San Francisco, CA: Jossey-Bass.

Smith, B. L., MacGregor, J., Matthews, R. S., & Gabelnick, F. (2004). *Learning communities: Reforming undergraduate education*. San Francisco, CA: Wiley.

Townsend, B. K., & Wilson, K. (2006). "A hand hold for a little bit": Factors facilitating the success of community college transfer students to a large research university. *Journal of College Student Development*, 47(4), 439–456.

JOHN E. FINK coordinates the Transfer2Terp Learning Community in the Adele H. Stamp Student Union at the University of Maryland.

MARY L. HUMMEL is assistant vice president for Student Affairs at the University of Maryland.

4

This chapter addresses strengths and difficulties encountered in implementing transfer learning community models and how efficacy is supported through transfer learning community programming. Transfer programming best practices and recommendations for program improvements are presented.

Aligning Needs, Expectations, and Learning Outcomes to Sustain Self-Efficacy Through Transfer Learning Community Programs

Jennifer R. Leptien

Increasing numbers of students are entering four-year institutions with community college credits and finding themselves void of well-integrated support for acclimation. Transfer students may find it difficult to transition from one institution to another due to increased institution and class sizes (Davies & Casey, 1999), and greater academic independence (Laanan, 1996). Many schools now collaborate to improve the rate of transfer from two-year to four-year institutions. One such collaboration is the creation of transfer articulation agreements. Handel (2007) describes the importance of a well-developed transfer articulation agreement in easing the transition from community college to the four-year institution. With increasing numbers of students transferring via these articulation agreements, it is important to consider how learning community programs may best assist students posttransfer so that the academic and social transition can be made as seamless as possible.

Learning communities provide small cohorts of students of similar academic interests with opportunities that may include taking two or more college courses together, forming study groups, and engaging in shared social and service activities with the guidance of learning community coordinators, peer mentors, and associated faculty and staff. Some communities of learners live together within the same residential hall or complex, while others meet only within the classroom or a common meeting space. Along with these benefits, cohort groups often have access to small group interactions with faculty and staff, and many receive additional academic and social

New Directions for Student Services, no. 149, Spring 2015 © 2015 Wiley Periodicals, Inc.
Published online in Wiley Online Library (wileyonlinelibrary.com) • DOI: 10.1002/ss.20116

support from upper division students in the same major or college who serve as peer mentors for the learning community (Laufgraben & Shapiro, 2004).

One of the greatest challenges in developing a learning community for transfer students is the diversity of coursework each student brings. In many cases, students may have already taken the introductory-level courses commonly linked to freshmen learning community programs, leaving few options to cluster students within the same courses. Additionally, the diversity of the students themselves may create difficulties in connecting them to one another. Some students may be commuting rather than living on campus, be of nontraditional age, be employed after class hours, be married, and/or have dependent children. Each of these circumstances influences their availability, or lack thereof, to engage in learning community activities.

Finding ways to address these issues presents both challenges and opportunities to those coordinating learning communities for transfer students, and the stories of those who have done this work deserve consideration. The following qualitative case study explores the experiences of learning community coordinators, including their understanding of the transfer experience and transfer programming design. The study focuses on the strengths and challenges encountered within transfer learning community design and how existing programming addresses efficacy and support among students. Learning community coordinators at the institution under study are full-time professional academic advisers, or program coordinators, who have been designated to develop and oversee the learning community program within their department or college. A focus group was conducted with transfer learning community coordinators, and program artifacts were analyzed to reveal the perceived needs of transfer students and understand what programmatic challenges may exist in meeting their needs. Additionally, focus group and artifact data were examined to better understand the support and development of self-efficacy provided within learning community programming. Through the lens of Bandura's (1994) four domains of self-efficacy, the analysis identifies areas that could be enhanced through adjustments in transfer learning community design.

Literature Review

Increasing numbers of students in higher education attend multiple institutions, with some moving in one direction, such as transferring from a two-year to a four-year institution, some "double-dipping" by attending two institutions at one time, while others "swirl" by moving back and forth between institutions (McCormick, 2003). Barriers for transfer students may include financial concerns, academic challenges, being socially disengaged at the university, inconsistency between self-ratings and abilities, lack of family support, and issues resulting from juggling multiple obligations such as attending to family responsibilities and working (Duggan & Pickering, 2008).

Research affirms the role of smaller class sizes in promoting greater student engagement, and learning communities provide a similar small-group opportunity for those students involved. In comparing community college to university experiences, Davies and Casey (1999) note that students who have transferred benefited from the smaller community college classroom environments; therefore, students transitioning to a large lecture classroom at the larger receiving institution may be at risk for being less engaged in the learning process. Additionally, students reported community college faculty and staff had a better understanding of and provided a more supportive environment for those juggling multiple roles at the community college than they did at the university (Davies & Casey, 1999). Greater student–faculty engagement has been supported to foster intellectual development, as well as to encourage academic autonomy among students (Chickering & Reisser, 1993). The works of Astin (1984) and Light (2001) highlight the importance of faculty interaction in determining student satisfaction with the college experience. Light (2001) asserts that faculty have the greatest influence when interweaving course content with the students' personal experiences and ways of knowing that can easily occur through the structure of a learning community.

Social support has been identified as a means for maintaining equilibrium throughout the transfer process. Davies and Casey (1999) found that those who were socially engaged at the university were more likely to report satisfaction with the campus environment, while those who were not socially connected reported feelings of distress and a lack of social support. Friendships and peer groups are known to promote self-esteem and expose students to diverse ways of thinking (Chickering & Reisser, 1993). Tinto (1987) underscores the importance of social connection by saying that:

> it is the daily interaction of the person with other members of the college in both the formal and informal academic and social domains of the college, and the person's perception or evaluation of the character of those interactions that in large measure determine decisions to staying or leaving (*sic*) [college]. (p. 127)

Frisby and Martin's (2010) findings indicate that interpersonal relationships among students, and between faculty and students, encouraged greater engagement within the classroom setting, and determined that student learning outcomes benefited most through the development of rapport with faculty. Townsend and Wilson's (2006) research reveals that transfer students desired study partners as a way to connect both academically and socially with others. Similarly, Chickering and Reisser (1993) report that collaborative student learning environments encourage greater engagement in the material covered in the classroom, as well as the development of caring relationships between students.

Conceptual Framework

Bandura's theory of self-efficacy (individuals' self-motivations and beliefs that they can achieve their goals) has served as a framework to define student behavior, performance, and persistence within the classroom (Wood & Locke, 1987; Zimmerman, 2000), to show how self-efficacy impacts the academic experience and persistence of first-year engineering students (Hutchison, Follman, Sumpter, & Bodner, 2006), and to guide efforts for supporting and enhancing classroom learning (Margolis & McCabe, 2006). This theory can also serve as a framework for evaluating student motivation. In particular, Bandura's (1994) four domains of efficacy—mastery experiences, vicarious experiences, social persuasion, and somatic/emotional influences—have provided a construct through which efficacy is measured in the academic context. Bandura's model closely aligns with the initiatives set forward by the learning community program at this study's site to acclimate students to the academic culture and to provide faculty–student engagement and academic support in an effort to retain students. The learning community approach has proven to be important for retaining students acclimating to the university (Baker & Pomerantz, 2000–2001; Hotchkiss, Moore, & Pitts, 2006; Johnson, 2000–2001). In a study by Coston, Lord, and Monell (2010), it was found that transfer stressors, such as navigating campus, work–school balance, concerns about major requirements, etc., were decreased over time through targeted intervention provided by a learning community experience.

While these studies demonstrate the utility of a learning community experience, little qualitative research exists to describe the benefits of learning community involvement for transfer students, the challenges of designing programs to meet the needs of this population, nor the extent to which self-efficacy is enhanced by learning community programming. This qualitative study investigated the accounts of transfer learning community coordinators to reveal the perceived needs of transfer students and the impact of learning community programming from the coordinator perspective.

Method

This study was conducted at Midwestern University, a large, Research I institution with existing transfer articulation agreements with all 15 in-state community colleges. Midwestern University has 80 separate learning communities serving over 4,700 undergraduate students. Of the 80 programs, seven learning communities have been developed specifically to serve transfer students. After receiving Institutional Review Board (IRB) approval, the researcher invited the coordinators who develop and implement the

Midwestern University transfer learning community programs to participate in a focus group to discuss transfer student transitions to the university and ways the coordinators engaged students through learning communities. The focus group interview, program artifacts, learning community program outcomes, and syllabi were transcribed, coded, and analyzed for overarching themes related to learning community programming.

Participants. Seven transfer-specific learning community programs at Midwestern University were analyzed within this study. The intended outcomes and learning community seminar syllabi from all seven programs were analyzed; however, only four individuals were able to participate in the coordinator focus group at week 13 of the study. The focus group participants had nearly 50 years of combined experience working with transfer students and had been coordinating each transfer learning community for a minimum of two years at the time of the study. Three of the coordinators were full-time academic advisers, and one coordinator was a full-time program coordinator at Midwestern University.

Procedures. Coordinators confirmed their willingness to participate and were invited to a 60-minute focus group, which was conducted at week 13 of the 15-week fall semester so that the coordinators could share experiences that had occurred throughout the semester and allow discussion of any projected changes, issues, and challenges that might be addressed before the semester's end. Individual learning community outcome documentation and syllabi supplemented the coordinator focus group transcripts. The coded data provide insight into the learning community components, identify how each of the components addresses an area within Bandura's (1994) four domains of efficacy, highlight the effectiveness of the components in meeting transfer student needs, identify what works and does not work for this population, and demarcate potential areas of improvement.

Results

The analysis of the data reveals three overarching themes in addressing the needs and challenges facing students in the transition from community college to the university. Bolstering academic performance, assisting in social integration, and developing career potential were clearly identified as needs of transfer students and thus foci of the learning community programs. The transfer learning community experience is viewed as a significant contributor to addressing these student needs, contributing to the success of the transfer students involved.

The coordinators report that their typical transfer students have jobs that require more work hours than incoming freshmen, are harder to engage outside of class, and have difficulties making connections with their peers. Challenges coordinators encountered in developing programs to address student needs are attributed to the variations among student needs and the need for more one-on-one attention. Enrolling the students in a learning community creates another obstacle for the coordinators. Course seat reservations are a notable challenge to this enrollment because there is a tendency for transfers to register for classes late, after seats held for learning community students have been released for use by the general student population. As well, there are problems with finding common courses to cluster for the incoming cohort; for example, some transfer students in an engineering learning community may have already received credit for the introductory math course that is paired with their introductory engineering course. In addition to these challenges, the coordinators identified that getting transfer student "buy-in" to the learning community is the greatest challenge. Coordinators feel that transfer students often do not see the value of the learning community experience until the semester is over. The coordinators' responses are unanimous in their assertion that transfer students most need academic support and assistance in their social integration to the new academic environment despite the sentiment that transfer students feel mature and question the need for learning community support. They also stress that transfer students have less time to plan and arrange internships since their matriculation at the university will be shortened in comparison to their traditional student peers. This puts the students at a potential disadvantage because if unaddressed, the students may need to lengthen their time to graduation.

Data were also examined to better understand the extent to which academic enhancement, social acclimation, and career development can be achieved by promoting students' efficacy. The efficacy framework was used as each of Bandura's (1994) four domains of self-efficacy (mastery experiences, vicarious experiences, social persuasion, and somatic/emotional influences) aligns with intended transfer learning community outcomes.

Academic Enhancement. The theme of academic enhancement was defined by the academic experiences enhancing mastery such as the integration of study groups, sharing and understanding academic resources, and knowledge of/participation in academic research. The intended learning outcomes articulated by the transfer learning community coordinators described the value of students helping one another to understand course content through study group participation. A second component of the learning community experience designed to enhance academic mastery is to make students aware of and direct them to academic resources, such as tutoring services and supplemental instruction, to develop their personal study skills and time management, and to make them aware of university policies and procedures. Another noted outcome was for the students to be aware of, and engage in, research opportunities within the institution. This was addressed through activities such as research presentations from faculty members and informing students of undergraduate research assistantships.

Coordinators described the importance of academic enhancement through mastery experiences. They explained that their transfer students tend to have high grade point averages at transfer and are often challenged by their high expectations about what they can handle during their first semester. Coordinator A explained:

> A lot of my students have really high GPAs and so their expectation is that "I'm in Honors and I have a 3.9 at the community college" and their expectations of "I can come here and take four core classes. . . ." [It's about] trying to get them to be more realistic in their expectations, trying to give them resources. We have study nights with them. Trying to get them to be more realistic about the reality. . . can you do this in exactly two years?

Being underprepared was reiterated by the other coordinators as well. Coordinator D reported:

> I saw that incoming transfer students were experiencing what I thought was pretty extreme difficulty academically. We did a study over several years and saw that the GPAs they had coming from community colleges especially would suffer significant drops the first year here and subsequently a lot of them would leave or be dismissed.

The opportunity for vicarious experiences to enhance student learning was evident in learning community documentation and coordinators' descriptions of students assisting one another with coursework and engaging in the academic experience as a transfer cohort. The learning community design presents an opportunity for the cohort to take one or more courses together and to be introduced to students who share the transfer experience. Assisting and learning from one another through study groups provide an environment through which the students can learn vicariously as a cohort.

Social persuasion was addressed in the intended learning outcomes by introducing faculty and staff to the students, motivating student engagement through team projects, and developing an engaging academic atmosphere. The learning community coordinators reported the importance of creating connections between the faculty, staff, and students to assist the students in their overall adjustment to the receiving institution. The development of these relationships and engagement in team activities were said to contribute to the students' sense of belonging. Coordinator C explained:

> It doesn't matter if it's a community college or a lateral transfer situation, just having come in later than that traditional first year experience really makes a difference for those that are going through it. They identify [with one another] because they've had different sorts of experiences.

The learning community coordinators expressed their desire to help students experience a smooth transition and decrease anxiety, which they noted commonly increases with changes in academic rigor from one institution to another. Assisting students' adaptation to changes in rigor, engaging them with other transfers in class, and helping them prepare for accelerated course content illustrate coordinators' concern and attention to the transfer students' somatic/emotional response to the transition. The learning community outcomes and syllabi included presentations about the assistance provided by the university student counseling program. Coordinators also encouraged mentors to share their transfer experiences in order to reassure the incoming class that they could persist through the transition. Coordinator D stated:

> I look for my peer mentors to be first and foremost role models so that they are involved and engaged. They are better than average academically. They've been successful so that they can model that behavior and they can explain things to them. They have to be good communicators and I always have at least one transfer student as a peer mentor. I don't know that the students treat them any differently in the classroom setting but I do know that individually when they meet with them, they tend to relate and talk about their previous experiences and it's almost like they're interpreters.

Social Acclimation. Social acclimation was evident in the intended learning community outcomes designed to allow students to contribute personal experiences to team projects, develop study groups, and enhance one another's learning experience. While study groups provide a clear academic benefit, they also provide a supportive social network for students as they encounter difficulties in the adjustment to the new academic culture. Additionally, friendships may develop, and the students benefit from learning from one another in this context. Networking is a noteworthy goal that learning communities intend to address.

In addition to providing opportunities for mastery experiences, social acclimation through student networking activities, residing among other transfer students, learning from their mentor's personal journey, and engaging in the university culture presented additional ways to engage in vicarious learning experiences through their integration with peers and the institution. One of the learning communities in the study offered a residential option wherein some of the learning community students lived among other transfer students. The value of knowing others encountering and addressing the same challenges was expected to provide a secondary layer of shared experiences among the students. While this was intended, it was not described as a critical outcome nor were specific student experiences explicated by coordinators connected to this study.

The sharing of a peer mentor's personal transfer story was described as an important tool for students to learn vicariously through their mentor's academic and social journey. The coordinators described how the students relied on their mentor's understanding of the transfer situation, and his/her personal story of persistence was a meaningful motivator for the incoming class. Additionally, the coordinators reported the value for transfer students of getting involved in extracurricular activities, previously noted as leading to satisfaction (Davies & Casey, 1999).

Social persuasion was addressed through the intent to create a comfortable environment in which students can ask questions, develop relationships with peers and mentors, and influence one another's opinion of the university and the overall academic experience. The coordinators sought to create environments in which the students would approach them with questions concerning their academic and social concerns. They noted the increased amount of time they had to spend individually working with their transfer students to help them better understand academic expectations and develop realistic goals in developing their graduation plans. They sought to build community among the students so they could get to know their mentors and one another through the integration of ice-breaker activities as well. The importance of social persuasion was articulated by Coordinator B:

> I think sometimes it takes a while for them to even acknowledge that they do have some similar needs [to incoming freshmen]. This year I [had students complete] their own self-assessment, and they talk about fitting in and getting to know their peers. Finding other students to study with and even some of them talk about homesickness. It's not as evident or significant with the transfer students as it is with freshmen, but I think it's harder for them to acknowledge because in their head, they're supposed to be further along and they're supposed to be able to make this transition. I think they have some of the same needs that freshmen do, it's just harder for them to acknowledge that.

Students' somatic or emotional responses were addressed by providing programming designed to increase their personal sense of well-being. These concerns were addressed through social activities in which the students could interact in an informal atmosphere and develop their sense of belonging within the learning community; however, the coordinators noted difficulties in engaging some students in these out-of-class activities. Coordinator D stated:

> You have people who maybe because they were at a community college, where it tends to be, not in all cases, but tends to be more of a commuter-based program. They don't feel a connection to that community college. I attended a local community college for a couple of years, on a part-time basis, and I didn't feel a part of that school. And I think they come here with the same mindset that I'm just gonna come here from such and such time to such and such time. Put in my time and coursework and then I'm off to my job for six or eight hours a day. I'll be back tomorrow or whatever convenient schedule they can get. That makes it really tough for them to be engaged.

Career Development. Career exploration and preparation are important elements of the college experience that were addressed by the focus group participants. Intended mastery experiences included acquiring skills necessary for the workplace and developing leadership potential. An example of this includes the integration of team projects and creating experiences in which the students can learn to work effectively as a team. The learning communities' intended outcomes included the importance of becoming effective communicators and gaining a thorough understanding of environmental and multicultural issues within their chosen field. Additionally, the students were provided opportunities to interview professionals in their chosen field, develop résumés and cover letters, identify career goals, and uncover job component details through career exploration assignments.

Vicarious career experiences were attended to in the transfer learning community outcomes via team projects, industry tours, field trips, and service-learning and community-service activities. Coordinator B reported:

> We also focus on out-of-class activities and service learning because I think that a lot of learning goes on outside the classroom, and I think you know how hard it is to get transfer students to do that. Seeking out leadership opportunities. . . we have them do a service learning project, with our peer mentors leading different groups. Obviously one of the outcomes in that is hoping they come out of that with some kind of feeling of civic responsibility, but also one of the main objectives is that they work with a smaller group of students on a project and hopefully build community.

Social persuasion in career development was intended to be influenced by student interaction with industry professionals and through student discovery of career options while in the learning community. Activities designed to engage and influence the students in this area included participating in mock interviews, meeting industry leaders while on field visits, and listening to presentations from faculty about career options within the major.

The goal of preparing transfer students for their future careers addressed somatic influences as well. It was intended that the students would be reassured and confident in their knowledge about their major, career options, and emergent issues within their chosen field. Additionally, experiences were planned to help prepare students for engaging in the career fair and encouraging them to think through their plans for attaining internships and co-ops. Coordinator C explained:

> I think something else especially with my population is there is a real sort of a quick get up to speed. You know they're, they need to get internships. They need to get work experience in their field. They need to get those leadership experiences, the soft skills that employers are looking for. And I think that's a real challenge to do in a short amount of time. . . . If we don't work to get them up to speed fast, they really miss out on some opportunities that employers are looking for, and so they maybe don't have all the advantages of a student that's been here from the first year, and I think it's difficult trying to get them to understand that sometimes.

Discussion

This study reiterated the value of providing mastery experiences such as study groups, knowledge about major requirements and university policies and procedures, and use of academic support services. Vicarious academic experiences were identified through cohort engagement and students assisting one another with schoolwork. Social persuasion through academic connections with faculty, staff, and other students was integrated into the design of the learning community. The learning communities incorporated opportunities for faculty to visit the learning community class and discuss their research as well. Based on existing research (Astin, 1984; Chickering & Reisser, 1993; Light, 2001), it is possible that this element could be better met with more intentional opportunities to engage with faculty outside of the classroom setting, such as the opportunity to dine with faculty, visit faculty research labs, and engage in fun activities like trivia nights. Providing support for coping with changes in academic rigor was an important goal for the learning community as well. Providing study group activities can support transfer student adjustment to increased rigor, offer networking opportunities, and meet social support needs.

Social acclimation was the second overarching goal of the learning communities in this study. The coordinators noted that it was more difficult to engage the students in social experiences due to competing demands from jobs and families. Additionally, one coordinator identified that many transfer students maintain a commuter approach to their university experience and thus are less engaged with the university in general. One way to mediate this is through additional active learning and networking opportunities, such as peer-to-peer teaching, within the learning community classroom experience. This could meet the students' need to know their classmates better without adding to the strain of returning to campus after class.

Career preparedness emerged as a theme within the learning community experience and is clearly connected to Bandura's (1994) domains of efficacy support. The importance of providing mastery experiences, such as those designed to enhance leadership and workplace skills, was integral to preparing transfer students for career fairs and internships. Furthermore, offering vicarious experiences, like service- and team-learning opportunities, and social persuasion through meeting industry professionals not only addressed somatic needs for reassurance of being in the correct major but also provided students with multiple opportunities to prepare for their future careers.

When prompted to suggest recommendations for starting a transfer learning community, coordinators identified several intended to improve transfer students' experiences. The first best practice was to ask students about their needs and uncover what they believe is missing throughout their first-semester experience. Secondly, they recommended avoiding a single model approach, noting that a first-year experience model may not work for this population due to variations in existing credits and outside obligations. They also described the importance of finding advocates in the administration to support the learning community's development and to involve faculty in any way possible for the benefit of the students. Systematically seeking feedback from students also is critical to program evaluation and helps to ascertain what works and what does not for them, from their perspective. And most importantly, the coordinators suggested new programs should start simple and grow in time. This allows the program to easily adapt to the changing needs of the students and provides flexibility for future growth.

Limitations

While this study provides an understanding about how the intended outcomes of learning communities address the efficacy of transfer students, more extensive exploration about how efficacy is influenced by learning community design and programming, the coordinators' perceptions and opinions regarding student efficacy, and the role of the coordinator in promoting student efficacy within each domain would be beneficial. Additionally, although outside the scope of this study, it would be helpful to engage coordinators and students in combined focus groups so that the students can share their emergent concerns with the coordinators themselves.

Implications for Future Research and Practice

This study was designed to inform transfer learning community programming and provides best practices for this growing population of students. The academic enhancement provided through learning community programming is essential to student efficacy because it influences emotional responses to the transition through enhancement of mastery and vicarious experiences. By facilitating the development of cohort experiences and study groups, and encouraging students to take advantage of academic support services, the learning community program is supporting and enhancing academic mastery at a transitional time when students' efficacy may be most threatened.

The study also highlights the important roles that peers, faculty, and staff play in the social acclimation of students to the university. It is recommended that learning community coordinators, administrators, and faculty seek out various ways to integrate students with faculty both inside and outside of the classroom so that students can experience a greater sense of connection to the university and build confidence as students and young professionals. This research supports that peer mentors have an opportunity to shape the student experience through role modeling. Mentors should be encouraged to share their personal academic journey for the benefit of the students they are mentoring. This encourages not only a deeper understanding of their academic path, but it is also a source of encouragement for the students who relate their own matriculation to the path of their mentor. Finally, career exploration and preparation were shown to be enhanced through learning community participation. By providing opportunities to explore careers in the major, developing internship and graduation plans, and engaging industry mentors in presentations, the learning community adds to the career mastery of its transfer students. This study demonstrates that each of these mastery and vicarious experiences is essential to the success of transfer learning community programs. It is recommended that these experiences, as well as providing an environment in which social persuasion and somatic influences are supported, should be integrated into future transfer learning community programs.

References

Astin, A. W. (1984). Student involvement: A developmental theory for higher education. *Journal of College Student Development*, *40*(5), 518–529.

Baker, S., & Pomerantz, N. (2000–2001). Impact of learning communities on retention at a Metropolitan University. *Journal of College Student Retention*, 2(2), 115–126.

Bandura, A. (1994). Self-efficacy. In V. S. Ramachandran (Ed.), *Encyclopedia of human behavior* (Vol. 4, pp. 71–81). New York, NY: Academic.

Chickering, A. W., & Reisser, L. (1993). *Education and identity* (2nd ed.). San Francisco, CA: Jossey-Bass.

Coston, C. T. M., Lord, V. B., & Monell, J. S. (2010). Improving the success of transfer students: Responding to risk factors. *Journal of Learning Communities Research*, *5*(2), 22–26.

Davies, T. G., & Casey, K. (1999). Transfer student experiences: Comparing their academic and social lives at the community college and university. *College Student Journal*, *33*(1), 60–70.

Duggan, M. H., & Pickering, J. W. (2008). Barriers to transfer student academic success and retention. *Journal of College Student Retention*, *9*(4), 437–459.

Frisby, B. N., & Martin, M. M. (2010). Instructor-student and student-student rapport in the classroom. *Communication Education*, *59*(2), 146–164.

Handel, S. J. (2007). Second chance, not second class: A blueprint for community-college transfer. *Change*, *39*(5), 38–45.

Hotchkiss, J. L., Moore, R. E., & Pitts, M. M. (2006). Freshman learning communities, college performance, and retention. *Education Economics*, *14*(2), 197–210.

Hutchison, M. A., Follman, D. K., Sumpter, M., & Bodner, G. M. (2006). Factors influencing the self-efficacy beliefs of first-year engineering students. *Journal of Engineering Education*, *95*(1), 39–47.

Johnson, J. (2000–2001). Learning communities and special efforts in the retention of university students: What works, what doesn't, and is the return worth the investment? *Journal of College Student Retention*, 2(3), 219–238.

Laanan, F. S. (1996). Making the transition: Understanding the adjustment process of community college transfer students. *Community College Review*, *23*(4), 69–81.

Laufgraben, J. L., & Shapiro, N. S. (2004). *Sustaining and improving learning communities*. San Francisco, CA: Jossey-Bass.

Light, R. J. (2001). *Making the most of college: Students speak their minds*. Cambridge, MA: Harvard University Press.

Margolis, H., & McCabe, P. P. (2006). Improving self-efficacy and motivation: What to do, what to say? *Intervention in School and Clinic*, *41*(4), 218–227.

McCormick, A. C. (2003). Swirling and double-dipping: New patterns of student attendance and their implications for higher education. In J. E. King, E. L. Anderson, & M. E. Corrigan (Eds.), *New Directions for Higher Education: No. 121. Changing student attendance patterns: Challenges for policy and practice* (pp. 13–24). San Francisco, CA: Jossey-Bass.

Tinto, V. (1987). *Leaving college: Rethinking the causes and cures of student attrition*. Chicago, IL: University of Chicago Press.

Townsend, B., & Wilson, K. (2006). "A hand hold for a little bit": Factors facilitating the success of community college transfer students to a large research university. *Journal of College Student Development*, 47(4), 439–456.

Wood, R. E., & Locke, E. A. (1987). The relation of self-efficacy and grade goals to academic performance. *Educational and Psychological Measurement*, 47(4), 1012–1024.

Zimmerman, B. J. (2000). Self-efficacy: An essential motive to learn. *Contemporary Educational Psychology*, 25(1), 82–91.

JENNIFER R. LEPTIEN has a PhD in human development and family studies and is a program coordinator for learning communities at Iowa State University.

5

In this chapter, the authors will expand upon the definition of learning communities, discussing the ways in which this concept has changed and adapted through the incorporation/infusion of web-based technologies. In addition, strategies on how to create and use online learning communities both with students and for professional practice will be shared.

Utilizing Online Learning Communities in Student Affairs

Daniel W. Calhoun, Lucy Santos Green

Online learning has improved access and availability to higher education for both traditional and nontraditional students. Today's traditional student shares many of the characteristics formerly associated with older, nontraditional learners: full-time employment, spouses and children, and elderly care or responsibilities (Roby, Ashe, Singh, & Clark, 2013). In order to reach this population, almost 90% of all higher education institutions today offer online courses. As a result, nearly half of all students who have graduated in the last 10 years have enrolled in at least one online course (Parker, Lenhart, & Moore, 2011). Even when overall enrollment numbers decline, as they have in recent years, online enrollments continue to rise. To illustrate the point, the overall enrollment growth rate in the fall academic terms of 2008, 2009, and 2010 was 4.7%, 2.2%, and 0.6%, respectively. During that same period, the enrollment growth rate of online students was 16.9%, 21.1%, and 10.1%, respectively (Britto & Rush, 2013).

Learning communities have and continue to be viewed as a successful intervention tool to aid students in their transition to college life (Renn & Reason, 2013). Considering the rise in online student enrollment and the changing demands faced by traditional students, as well as job market expectations for technological literacy, it is imperative that we utilize technology-enhanced learning communities to support student success. As we progress through the second decade of the 21st century, the field of student affairs has the opportunity to recognize and embrace the potential of technology to expand on the proven success of the learning community structure. In fact, the benefits of learning communities are present regardless of the delivery format, be it face-to-face, blended, or fully online (Lenning, Hill, Saunders, Solan, & Stokes, 2013).

NEW DIRECTIONS FOR STUDENT SERVICES, no. 149, Spring 2015 © 2015 Wiley Periodicals, Inc.
Published online in Wiley Online Library (wileyonlinelibrary.com) • DOI: 10.1002/ss.20117

While the merits of learning communities within student affairs have been discussed throughout this volume, the incorporation of technology into higher education today leads us to ask—how do we effectively utilize web-based technologies to bring learning communities into the digital age? In this chapter, we will delve into the concept of online learning communities (OLCs), theories behind OLCs, and ways in which student affairs professionals can best use these structures to serve students today.

Defining and Describing Online Learning Communities

Learning communities have been implemented in colleges and universities across the United States in hopes of providing a holistic student collegiate experience, promoting cross-curricular connections, and increasing student retention rates (Love, 2012). Snyder (2009) defines a learning community as a group of people who possess a common interest in learning and sharing knowledge. Even so, a clear-cut definition of a learning community is difficult to find. Smith, MacGregor, Matthews, and Gabelnick (2004) describe learning communities in terms of models and structures, such as freshman interest groups and gateway courses. However, it is this elasticity that enables different organizations to invent institution-specific models—some of these based on or adapted from other designs (Ellertson & Thoennes, 2007). Regardless of a learning community's structure, it is its joint focus on both intellectual development and socially embedded learning that help its participants explore deeply interconnected academic curriculum in more authentic ways (Snyder, 2009; Tinto, Goodsell, & Russo, 1994).

Considering the popularity and ubiquity of both learning communities and online learning platforms, it is only natural that these structures have expanded into the digital realm, becoming OLCs. Over the past five years, student affairs staff have taken on instructor roles in OLCs, such as first-year experience or orientation courses, communities that aim to introduce students to campus life or to a specific major (Ellertson & Thoennes, 2007). An OLC is a digital version of a learning community in that it brings together students, faculty, student affairs professionals, and other institutional members who interact and connect with each other within a learning management system (Blanchard & Cook, 2012; Lenning et al., 2013).

Through restricted access, online discussion tools and web 2.0 technologies, online platforms are now able to promote feelings of trust, respect, and connection among members, feelings vital to the maintenance of learning communities (West, 2010). It is also important to note that there is a distinct difference between online communities, informal spaces where individuals with common interests gather, and online *learning* communities (OLCs), formal spaces that promote "collaborative learning and the reflective practice involved in transformative learning" (Oliver, Herrington, Herrington, & Reeves, 2007, p. 4).

In addition, despite the robustness of technology tools, there are differences between online and face-to-face learning communities. Perhaps the most distinctive differences are evident in communication. While VOIP (voice over internet protocol) technologies such as Skype and Google+ Hangout allow for real-time visual exchanges, the majority of discussions in OLCs are conducted through text. These conversations may happen synchronously (through chat tools), or, as is most often the case, asynchronously (through discussion board posts), lasting over the course of several days (West, 2010). The visible and permanent record of these exchanges further impacts communication in OLCs, allowing for deeper reflection on member ideas and contributions.

Designing Online Learning Communities

A common misconception, a *Field of Dreams* mentality, revolves around the building of OLCs. This misconception assumes "if we build it, they will come," an idea born out of the belief that interactive technology tools and feature-rich learning management systems have special and engaging characteristics that automatically establish a functioning OLC. Blanchard and Cook (2012) warn that an emphasis on technology versus design "can easily lead to wasted time and effort for anyone developing an [online learning community]" (p. 93). Rather, research on design of OLCs, and online courses in general, continually states that learning design and pedagogical choices are the most significant factors in the creation of community (Green, Inan, & Denton, 2012; Liu, Magjuka, Bonk, & Lee, 2007).

Previously in this chapter, we pointed out the flexibility of learning communities, and how this flexibility lends itself to the implementation of unique models and approaches that are institution specific (Lenning et al., 2013). Flexibility is an important component of the concept of learning communities and should not be hampered by templates or strict design prescripts. Even so, there are general characteristics that are of critical importance in the establishment of rich and thriving OLCs. In this section, we highlight the following characteristics: learning design, facilitation for online communication, and interactive technologies.

Learning Design. When designing learning experiences, whether online or face-to-face, there are several assumptions that can be made about the average adult learner. First, as people mature, they transition from being extrinsically motivated learners to intrinsically motivated learners. Intrinsically motivated learners have a strong need to know the "why" behind learning new material, place a high value on life experiences as learning resources, and demonstrate a preference for information that is immediately relevant to one's daily life (Snyder, 2009). Learning design for the intrinsically motivated incorporates tasks that encourage learners to examine information and materials from multiple viewpoints, both practical and theoretical, drawing upon a broad range of personal and academic resources (Bransford, Vye, Kinzer, & Risko, 1990). Most importantly, these are tasks designed to replicate, as much as possible, the real-world activities of practicing professionals as opposed to decontextualized classroom exercises (Brown, Collins, & Duguid, 1989).

Second, and this parallels the transition from extrinsic to intrinsic motivation for learning, adult learners (even young adult learners) shift from a dependent personality toward a more self-directed personality (Snyder, 2009). This characteristic calls for the design of learning experiences that "acknowledge differing learner needs, abilities, and interests; affording personal control and choice to learners" (Roby et al., 2013, p. 30). Note that in an online environment, learner preference can easily be supported through the creation and delivery of multimodal (text, audio, and visual) content. Tasks and interactive learning experiences that include learner choice include this consideration in their outcomes by allowing for multiple, and sometimes competing/contrasting, solutions versus a single expected outcome. Additionally, self-directed learners should be provided with the opportunity to reflect on the learning choices they make, both privately and within the learning community itself, either through task logs, online journal and discussion posts, or short video blogs—activities embedded within the tasks themselves (Oliver et al., 2007).

Third, learning design for young and mature adults acknowledges an evolution in learner orientation from content-centered to problem-centered tasks (Snyder, 2009). In problem-centered tasks, learners are required to define a problem, identify and prioritize subtasks, and work toward a self- or group-identified solution over a longer period of time, whether days, weeks, or months (Bransford et al., 1990). This is not to say that problem-centered tasks take away from any content mastery the OLC is attempting to promote. In fact, problem-centered tasks encourage deeper and more robust learning because while engaging with the problem, learners take on multiple roles, developing an interdisciplinary perspective rather than limiting content mastery to one topic, field, or domain (Jonassen, 1999).

Finally, it is worth considering that problem-centered tasks are opportunities for OLCs to engage members in service learning, a pedagogical approach that has been shown to promote student leadership development, improved academic performance, and rich learning experiences (Love, 2012). For example, OLC members can brainstorm solutions to a general community problem (service opportunity) online and implement solutions individually in their own locations. Members then reflect on the service-learning component with their OLC through discussion posts, chats, or video blogs.

Online Communication and Trust Building. Learning is oftentimes described as a social endeavor, a process that occurs through continuous conversation, social networks, and community-based practices. When learners are completing learning tasks, they typically turn to conversations and informal social networks for information and help. Amazingly, research has determined that people would rather exchange information with those who are most accessible over those who are most qualified (Cadima, Ojeda, & Monguet, 2012). Communication and trust, critical ingredients of the social learning process, need to be carefully structured and fostered in an online learning environment. As previously mentioned in this chapter, communication in OLCs (which can happen both synchronously and asynchronously) and consequently, trust building, reflects one of the most distinct differences between online and face-to-face learning communities.

When designers develop OLCs that encourage learner interaction, the strength and success of that community oftentimes depend on the quality of those interactions. This is because a successful OLC develops a group identity—a process that cannot occur without its members first learning about one another, sharing individual identities with each other, and eventually trusting one another (Postmes, Spears, Lee, & Novak, 2005). Trust is considered a key enabler for communication in OLCs (Fang & Chiu, 2010). However, the online platform can oftentimes strip communication of trust-building ingredients: facial expressions, verbal and nonverbal cues. In order to address this challenge, there are several strategies that can be implemented: (a) encourage members to post detailed personal profiles; (b) promote interactive profiles with the use of web 2.0 tools that include video and audio capability such as Glogster or VoiceThread; and (c) establish an off-topic discussion board, an online café, and encourage the posting of pictures and short video or audio responses (Jones et al., 2012). As an additional benefit, members who share both personal and professional information about themselves with the community help build trust by allowing the OLC to better gauge their expertise (Booth, 2012).

Recall the metaphor of the *Field of Dreams* in the design and launch of an OLC. One may implement the suggested strategies at the onset of the OLC, but if trust building and communication within the OLC is not continuously monitored, pruned, and maintained, learner interaction may taper off and disappear altogether. Communication is most likely to occur if OLCs avail themselves of one or several members or instructors who "encourage perspective taking, define norms and expectations, model appropriate communications, foster substantive interaction, provide relevant resources, and define roles and responsibilities for collaborative work" (Beach, 2012, p. 259). These instructors or members function as moderators, facilitators, and monitors.

The individuals chosen to fulfill these roles may vary depending on the structure and design of the OLC and the needs of its participants. Some OLC instructors call on members to individually serve in each of these roles. Instructors often select these members based on previous OLC experience and instructor–member relationships (Booth, 2012). Other OLC instructors prefer to assume all three roles. This option tends to be utilized in OLCs consisting of students who are new to the college experience or unfamiliar with online platforms.

Moderators. The job of a moderator is to seed discussions and to scaffold structured conversations. He or she works to move communication exchanges beyond the superficial (Booth, 2012). Much of the work of the moderator happens behind the scenes. This individual may help shape knowledge by modifying or building upon existing posts; however, he or she does not contribute original ideas. Instead, the moderator pushes the OLC forward by comparing and contrasting learner perspectives, reconciling areas of commonality, and questioning stark differences. In this manner, he or she provides support, as well as a model, for members who would like to take on more leadership within the OLC. Moderators also help new community members integrate into the OLC by pushing all learners (regardless of initial level of participation) to contribute (Singh & Holt, 2013).

Facilitators. The facilitator affirms and encourages participation. In several ways, the facilitator can be described as a servant leader who highlights the value in member contributions, gently guiding learners into a state of interdependency and reciprocity (Bunt-Kokhuis & Sultan, 2012). The role of the facilitator involves motivating and inspiring all learners to engage in successful dialogue. Booth (2012) logged a motivating email sent by Henry, an OLC's facilitator, to a member: "Charles, I'd like to tell you how much I enjoy your thoughtful posts. You've become an important member of the community. Keep up the good work" (p. 15). Facilitators carefully connect the content and topic of the OLC to the individual context and cultural backgrounds of the OLC's members. In making these connections, facilitators guide members through the process of reading and interpreting messages online in such a way that members become critical online listeners—"aware of filters such as biases, judgments and attitudes that affect how they interpret messages" (West, 2010, p. 72). Through critical online listening, OLC members develop the ability to assess the applicability of their own ideas and assumptions in relation to others in the community, building a shared sense of meaning and community values (Bunt-Kokhuis & Sultan, 2012).

Monitors. Paul, an OLC member, described the importance of his community's monitor: "People need to feel they can be together and carry on with their social discourse without fear of attack. When people come into the community with 'their guns a blazing' he has to be the sheriff. That is a critical part of sustaining trust to me" (Booth, 2012, p. 17). As evidenced in Paul's description, a monitor is mostly concerned with helping members maintain appropriate and trustworthy online behavior. This can be accomplished in several ways. The monitor should take the time to clearly explain the rules of online communication, going so far as to post a community's netiquette policy where it is easily accessed and reviewed. The monitor might work with the OLC members to jointly develop communication policy and procedures, a choice that can empower members to take ownership and responsibility for their own online behavior (Bunt-Kokhuis & Sultan, 2012).

Others have found it beneficial to create and share monthly newsletters that remind OLC members of those policies, as well as the overall learning goals for that community.

Interactive Technologies. Those new to online learning and learning management systems are typically very concerned with functional and technical issues (Green et al., 2012). Because technology is the mediator and principal vehicle in an OLC, the way members engage with technology—and how successful they feel in that engagement—can have profound consequences for the development of a sense of community (West, 2010). Therefore, the selection of technology tools and how these are employed are important considerations in the design of OLCs. When selecting technology tools, consider that online materials should support diverse presentation methods, multimodal content, learner preference and control, and collaborative, electronic exchange.

Technology changes at a rapid pace and keeping up with newer tools can be a daunting task. In addition, learning management system tools can be cumbersome, while paid-for software like Adobe Connect might disappear when institutional funding is rerouted. Free and open-source web 2.0 technologies are an attractive solution to these issues and can be used by OLC members even after their participation concludes (Jones et al., 2012). We have compiled a list of the more commonly used tools at our own institution. Although the recommended list below is by no means exhaustive or appropriate for every OLC or student affairs professional, they represent a starting point for exploration. We encourage the selection of one or two for inclusion in each new iteration of an OLC so that no designer or learner is overburdened with technology concerns.

- Curation and personal learning networks: RebelMouse, Scoop.it, Flipboard, and Zite.
- Digital storytelling: VoiceThread and Animoto.
- Electronic storage: Google Drive, Dropbox, and Evernote.
- Interactive images: ThingLink, Voki, and Blabberize.
- Open source learning management systems: Edmodo, Google+, and Schoology.
- Polling: Polldaddy, Google Forms, and SurveyMonkey.
- Screencasting: Screencast-O-Matic and Jing.
- Video playlists: YouTube and Mag.ma.
- Voice over Internet Protocol (VOIP): Skype, Google+ Hangout with Calendar feature.
- Wikis and website creators: PB Wiki, Weebly, SnapPages, Google Sites.

Most of the tools listed above have collaborative features, can be combined with other web 2.0 technologies for enhancement of those features, come in both free and pro options, and are available as mobile applications for both iOS and Android platforms.

Benefits of Online Learning Communities in Student Affairs

Learning communities help students engage with each other and with university life and culture by integrating members both socially and academically into the institutional environment (Tinto, 1997, 2004). OLCs function in much the same way, offering similar advantages to students and student affairs professionals.

Establishing a Sense of Community. Students who feel connected to the institution are more likely to remain at that institution (Allen, Robbins, Casillas, & Oh, 2008; Harris, 2006–2007; Tinto, 1997, 2004). Participation in OLCs requires students to have regular interaction with many members of the academy, cementing connections that inherently serve as a retention tool. Those within OLCs have the luxury of nurturing community connections asynchronously: anytime and anywhere, without the constraints of time, situation, or place. OLCs offer the flexibility that residential or campus-based learning communities do not. For commuters, fully online students, or those attending community colleges, OLCs provide a means of connection for students who might not otherwise participate.

Involvement in an OLC serves as a way for students to connect to the university as a whole, and individually to faculty members, staff, and peers, whether they are physically on campus or not. These connections, defined as *closeness centrality*, are crucial to knowledge construction, resource sharing, and the exchange of tacit or implicit information (Hansen, 2002). OLCs provide the proximity and close, trusting relationships needed to reduce feelings of isolation and loneliness often felt by students (Liu et al., 2007; Nicpon et al., 2006–2007). Closeness centrality developed in OLCs also can lead to academic confidence. Liu et al. (2007) reported that when OLC students indicated feeling a strong sense of community, they also perceived themselves to be more engaged, satisfied, and successful in their own learning.

Enhancing Student Learning. Students involved in OLCs can help each other to acquire and retain knowledge. Information shared at a campus program or meeting is delivered to students all at once. For some students, this method of delivery may not be ideal, as it is easy for details to be missed or lost. Those who are not able to attend these meetings may miss out on valuable information.

In OLCs that operate asynchronously, students have the ability to review a video, reread an online chart, or retake a test, accessing materials and asking questions at their own pace—a strong advantage for international and English language learner student populations, for example. They also can read the questions and responses of others and incorporate those ideas into their own learning. OLCs deliver information in multimodal ways (text, audio, and video), while online platforms allow for the integration of universal learning principles. Therefore, involvement in OLCs supports students of varied learning preferences and abilities.

OLCs provide students with high accessibility to those who can help aid in learning and knowledge acquisition. They offer students a chance to access these resources and information under the guidance and tutelage of their peers and student affairs mentors. For students who may be afraid to ask a question, or who may not know what questions to ask, this setting is especially helpful. Students get the answers they need in a low-risk environment, while both faculty and student affairs professionals feel a part of the process in a noninvasive way. OLCs are settings "in which student affairs professionals can explicitly demonstrate their roles as facilitators of student learning and partners in the educational process—that is, as teachers" (Ellertson & Thoennes, 2007, p. 35).

Professional Online Learning Communities. While the focus of this chapter is on OLCs as they pertain to students, we would be remiss if we failed to mention OLC opportunities for student affairs professionals and faculty members. While not directly involving students, the benefits that OLCs bring to faculty and staff impact students in multiple ways.

Online professional learning communities serve as a forum for professionals to network and collaborate both socially and professionally (Beach, 2012). The existence of places for professionals to share ideas in a structured way on a variety of topics is extremely beneficial and has a positive effect on both knowledge and practice (Beach, 2012; Masters, de Kramer, O'Dwyer, Dash, & Russell, 2010). Members of professional OLCs are able to "continually inquire into their practice and, as a result, discover, create, and negotiate new meanings that improve their practice..." (National Council of Teachers of English, 2010, p. 1). For example, a professional learning community could be created around the topic of crisis intervention. Members of the professional OLC could share experiences around a specific crisis, which in turn is available for other members to utilize at their discretion. Members available for consultation can help clarify issues and concerns about that topic. Professional products such as documents, strategies, and tools, uniquely tailored to the needs of the profession, are generated. These materials "have increased meaning because the explicit knowledge requires the tacit knowledge inherent in the community to be applied" (Booth, 2012, p. 5). Similarly, since OLCs are self-contained and only accessible to members, they provide a safe space for student affairs staff to reflect and try out new ideas and practices (Beach, 2012).

Conclusion

This chapter has introduced the idea of OLCs and explored how these can be developed and utilized in student affairs settings. Technology is a part of today's higher education learning environment, whether a student lives on campus, in town, in another state, or in another country. As student affairs professionals we should create, monitor, and maintain OLCs, instilling in members a sense of history filled with common interests and shared pride. As the gatekeepers and guides of OLCs, we should, through our own example, encourage members to participate and actively engage with each other. We should create and participate in professional OLCs, so that we can also benefit from mutual support and guidance in order to provide the best learning experiences for our students. The more comfortable we become with using technology and the tools and affordances it makes available, the better equipped we are to lead our students in their pursuit of lifelong learning in the 21st century.

References

Allen, J., Robbins, S. B., Casillas, A., & Oh, I. (2008). Third-year college retention and transfer: Effects of academic performance, motivation, and social connectedness. *Review of Higher Education*, *49*, 647–664.

Beach, R. (2012). Can online learning communities foster professional development? *Language Arts*, *89*(4), 256–262.

Blanchard, A. L., & Cook, J. R. (2012). Virtual learning communities centered within a discipline: Future directions. In K. Buch & K. E. Barron (Eds.), *New Directions for Teaching and Learning: No. 132. Discipline-centered learning communities: Creating connections among students, faculty, and curricula* (pp. 85–97). San Francisco, CA: Jossey-Bass.

Booth, S. E. (2012). Cultivating knowledge sharing and trust in online communities for educators. *Journal of Educational Computing Research*, *47*(1), 1–31.

Bransford, J. D., Vye, H., Kinzer, C., & Risko, V. (1990). Teaching thinking and content knowledge: Toward an integrated approach. In B. F. Jones & L. Idol (Eds.), *Dimensions of thinking and cognitive instruction* (pp. 381–413). Hillsdale, NJ: Lawrence Erlbaum Associates.

Britto, M., & Rush, S. (2013). Developing and implementing comprehensive student support services for online students. *Journal of Asynchronous Learning Networks*, *17*(1), 29–42.

Brown, J. S., Collins, A., & Duguid, P. (1989). Situated cognition and the culture of learning. *Educational Researcher*, *18*(1), 32–42.

Bunt-Kokhuis, S., & Sultan, N. (2012). Servant-leadership: The online way! E-learning where community building is key. *European Journal of Open, Distance and E-Learning*, *1*. Retrieved from http://www.eurodl.org/materials/contrib/2012/van-de-Bunt-Kokhuis_Sultan.pdf

Cadima, R., Ojeda, J., & Monguet, J. M. (2012). Social networks and performance in distributed learning communities. *Educational Technology & Society*, *15*(4), 296–304.

Ellertson, S., & Thoennes, K. V. (2007). Reframing teaching and learning: Lessons from learning communities for student affairs. In E. L. Moore (Ed.), *New Directions for Student Services: No. 117. Student affairs staff as teachers* (pp. 35–46). San Francisco, CA: Jossey-Bass.

Fang, Y. H., & Chiu, C. M. (2010). In justice we trust: Exploring knowledge-sharing continuance intentions in online communities of practice. *Computers in Human Behavior*, *26*, 235–246.

Green, L., Inan, F. A., & Denton, B. (2012). Examination of factors impacting student satisfaction with a new learning management system. *Turkish Online Journal of Distance Education*, *13*(3), 189–197. Retrieved from http://eric.ed.gov/?id=EJ997816

Hansen, M. T. (2002). Knowledge networks: Explaining effective knowledge sharing in multiunit companies. *Organization Science*, *13*(3), 232–248.

Harris, B. (2006–2007). The importance of creating a 'Sense of Community.' *Journal of College Student Retention: Research, Theory & Practice*, *8*(1), 83–105.
Jonassen, D. (1999). Designing constructivist learning environments. In C. M. Reigeluth (Ed.), *Instructional-design theories and models: A new paradigm of instructional theory* (Vol. II, pp. 215–239). Mahwah, NJ: Lawrence Erlbaum Associates.
Jones, S., Green, L. S., Hodges, C. B., Kennedy, K., Downs, E., Repman, J., & Clark, K. (2012). Supplementing the course management system: Using Web 2.0 for collaboration, communication and productivity in the preparation of school technology leaders. In D. Polly, C. Mims, & K. Persichitte (Eds.), *Developing technology-rich teacher education programs: Key issues* (pp. 118–134). Hershey, PA: IGI Global.
Lenning, O. T., Hill, D. M., Saunders, K. P., Solan, A., & Stokes, A. (2013). *Powerful learning communities: A guide to developing student, faculty and professional learning communities to improve student success and organizational effectiveness*. Sterling, VA: Stylus.
Liu, X., Magjuka, R. J., Bonk, C. J., & Lee, S. (2007). Does a sense of community matter? An examination of participants' perceptions of building learning communities in online courses. *The Quarterly Review of Distance Education*, *8*(1), 9–24.
Love, A. G. (2012). The growth and current state of learning communities in higher education. In K. Buch & K. E. Barron (Eds.), *New Directions for Teaching and Learning: No. 132. Discipline-centered learning communities: Creating connections among students, faculty, and curricula* (pp. 5–18). San Francisco, CA: Jossey-Bass.
Masters, J., de Kramer, R., O'Dwyer, L. M., Dash, S., & Russell, M. (2010). The effects of online professional development on fourth grade English language arts teachers' knowledge and instructional practices. *Journal of Educational Computing Research*, *43*(3), 355–375.
National Council of Teachers of English. (2010). *Teacher learning communities: A policy research brief*. Retrieved from http://www.ncte.org/library/NCTEFiles/Resources/Journals/CC/0202-nov2010/CC0202Policy.pdf
Nicpon, M., Huser, L., Blanks, E., Sollenberger, S., Befort, C., & Kurpius, S. (2006–2007). The relationship of loneliness and social support with college freshmen's academic performance and persistence. *Journal of College Student Retention: Research, Theory & Practice*, *8*(3), 345–358.
Oliver, R., Herrington, A., Herrington, J., & Reeves, T. C. (2007). Representing authentic learning designs supporting the development of online communities of learners. *Journal of Learning Design*, 2(2), 1–21.
Parker, K., Lenhart, A., & Moore, K. (2011). *The digital revolution and higher education: College presidents, public differ on value of online learning*. Washington, DC: Pew Social and Demographic Trends, Pew Research Center. Retrieved from http://files.eric.ed.gov/fulltext/ED524306.pdf
Postmes, T., Spears, R., Lee, A. T., & Novak, R. J. (2005). Individuality and social influence in groups: Inductive and deductive routes to group identity. *Journal of Personality and Social Psychology*, *89*(5), 747–763.
Renn, K. A., & Reason, R. D. (2013). *College students in the United States: Characteristics, experiences, and outcomes*. San Francisco, CA: Jossey-Bass.
Roby, T., Ashe, S., Singh, N., & Clark, C. (2013). Shaping the online experience: How administrators can influence student and instructor perceptions through policy and practice. *The Internet and Higher Education*, *17*(1), 29–37.
Singh, V., & Holt, L. (2013). Learning and best practices for learning in open-source software communities. *Computers & Education*, *63*, 98–108.
Smith, B. L., MacGregor, J., Matthews, R. S., & Gabelnick, F. (2004). *Learning communities: Reforming undergraduate education*. San Francisco, CA: Wiley.
Snyder, M. M. (2009). Instructional-design theory to guide the creation of online learning communities for adults. *TechTrends*, *53*(1), 48–56.

Tinto, V. (1997). Classrooms as communities: Exploring the educational character of student persistence. *Journal of Higher Education*, *68*, 599–623.
Tinto, V. (2004). Linking learning and leaving: Exploring the role of the college classroom in student departure. In J. M. Braxton (Ed.), *Reworking the student departure puzzle* (pp. 81–94). Nashville, TN: Vanderbilt University Press.
Tinto, V., Goodsell, A., & Russo, P. (1994). *Building learning communities for new college students*. State College: National Center on Postsecondary Teaching, Learning, and Assessment, Pennsylvania State University.
West, R. (2010). A student's guide to strengthening an online community. *TechTrends*, *54*(5), 69–75.

DANIEL W. CALHOUN is an assistant professor of higher education administration at Georgia Southern University.

LUCY SANTOS GREEN is an assistant professor of instructional technology at Georgia Southern University.

6

For a number of learning community programs, peer mentors provide an additional layer of staffing support. This chapter highlights peer mentor roles from a sample of programs and suggests important components for the construction of these roles.

Utilizing Peer Mentor Roles in Learning Communities

Laura Jo Rieske, Mimi Benjamin

With the many and varied goals of different learning communities, it is not surprising that the staffing structure of these programs varies as well. At the student staff level, many learning community programs rely on paraprofessional staff members, often referred to in the broadest sense as "peer mentors," to provide assistance to students and address the goals of the program. According to Miller, Groccia, and Miller (2001), "peer groups play an important role in influencing adolescent motivation, beliefs, engagement, and achievement. Peers exert influence through socialization processes involving information exchange, modeling, and reinforcement of peer norms and values both inside and outside the classroom" (p. xvi). As a result, peers can have a significant impact on other students' learning experiences, making the use of peers in settings such as learning communities a logical choice.

This chapter focuses on peer mentor roles, with specific attention to peer mentors in learning communities, by identifying the limited information available about such roles, highlighting examples from a sample of learning community programs, and noting commonalities as well as valuable elements from each. The information may provide new ideas for those currently utilizing peer mentors in their learning communities and may offer suggestions for those considering incorporating student mentors.

What Are Peer Mentors?

The concept of peer mentors has evolved over time and so has its definition. There is not a standard understanding of the function of peer mentors in higher education because peer mentors at different institutions have different responsibilities; there is no consistent definition of mentoring (Jacobi, 1991). In fact, much of the literature on peer mentors simply notes

NEW DIRECTIONS FOR STUDENT SERVICES, no. 149, Spring 2015 © 2015 Wiley Periodicals, Inc.
Published online in Wiley Online Library (wileyonlinelibrary.com) • DOI: 10.1002/ss.20118

that there is limited research on peer mentors, particularly those working with learning communities. Student affairs practitioners may benefit from a framework and a common language to describe and enhance peer mentor roles. Similarities within mentoring programs can lead to a more consistent definition, which ultimately can help researchers make more accurate comparisons across various mentoring programs (Gershenfeld, 2014).

Although previous research has identified multiple definitions of mentoring as a limitation, we attempt to merge those ideas to highlight existing peer mentor programs, first in general and then specifically, as related to learning communities. Peer mentors are role models (Jacobi, 1991) who often have valuable wisdom, which they gained from experience (Merriam, 1983). The primary role of peer mentors is to aid others in their successful transition to college by providing academic and emotional support (Gershenfeld, 2014; Minor, 2007).

Various peer mentor roles exist across institutions of higher education. Orientation leaders are dedicated to helping new students successfully transition to college. Peer advisors assist faculty in providing academic advising to other students. Similarly, tutors provide academic support to their peers by providing supplemental education to students outside of the classroom. In fraternity and sorority culture, mentoring occurs between an older class of members and a newer class to aid in the adjustment to the organization. Resident assistants foster the development of students by encouraging a safe and interactive community within the residence halls. Each of these roles has different functional responsibilities, but they share the common goal of providing support to peers.

Why Are Peer Mentors Valuable?

There are many benefits of peer mentoring programs for both the students who are being mentored, the students in the peer mentor roles, and the institution generally. The academic and social support that peer mentors provide is beneficial to the target group of students (Minor, 2007), and peer mentors can assist students in further connecting to the institution by encouraging academic and social involvement (Colvin & Ashman, 2010). Peer mentors are important student leaders who help increase interactions and involvement on campus, which are significant contributors to student retention (Tinto, 1986), a valuable factor for both students and institutions of higher education. Similarly, living-learning centers, social interaction, and academic adjustment have positive effects on student achievement (Pascarella & Terenzini, 2005), so peer-to-peer interactions in learning communities that provide academic support may be particularly helpful for student success.

The benefits of peer education extend beyond academic support and student involvement. While Astin (1984) has noted the important influence of peers in higher education, Newton and Ender (2010) offer particular benefits of these roles to the mentors:

> college students who participate in peer education display significant improvements in leadership, gain interpersonal communication skills, increase peer-education relevant knowledge, develop higher levels of self-esteem, and create better health behaviors when measured on assessments before and after their peer education experience. (p. 13)

Overall, peer mentors are valuable to college students and institutions of higher education because their services contribute to students' academic and social support, retention, and academic achievement.

Some significant advantages for peer mentors are related to student involvement. Astin (1984) theorized that student involvement—the degree of energy that students dedicate to their college experience—is related to student learning. College students who hold leadership positions, like peer mentor roles, benefit from the quality of that involvement. Specifically, peer mentors are educated through trainings, supervision meetings, and experience, which help them develop leadership skills, gain experience, and contribute to the community (Minor, 2007; Newton & Ender, 2010). They also develop connections and are able to apply concepts they learn through their experiences as peer mentors to their own lives (Colvin & Ashman, 2010).

Additionally, peer mentors provide a valuable and affordable service to the institution. Given the economic pressures on colleges and universities, using peer mentors can be a smart fiscal decision as the costs of employing students are typically less than those associated with hiring additional professional staff. As Sampson and Cohen (2001) noted, "Peer learning does not place significant demands on resources" (p. 32). While many peer mentor positions are paid roles, others may be volunteer leadership opportunities that can be attractive to students who hope to gain additional skills through the experience.

For the purposes of this chapter, we offer general peer mentor role descriptions and examples and then move to the peer mentor role descriptions focused specifically on learning communities. These examples were selected because they demonstrate multiple institutional and programmatic types and highlight the various responsibilities of peer mentor roles.

General Peer Mentor Roles

This section provides examples of peer mentor roles within various contexts in higher education.

Getting Engaged in Mentoring Students (GEMS) at Saint Peter's University. In Saint Peter's University's First Year Experience program (Saint Peter's University First Year Experience, 2012), the Getting Engaged in Mentoring Students (GEMS) peer mentors focus on engaging first-year students academically. GEMS foster student and community engagement by assisting with a freshman seminar course, meeting with students to help them understand coursework and homework, and supporting campus activities/events (N. Decapua, personal communication, March 20, 2014). In order to be eligible for the GEMS position, students must have at least 30 credits and a minimum GPA of 2.50. Students are selected based on their successful interview with the Dean of Freshmen and Sophomores and the First Year Experience and Student Engagement Coordinator. GEMS are expected to take the initiative to connect with students (through such efforts as meeting students in their residence halls and working with students in the tutoring center), help students prepare for major assignments and exams, and ensure that the first-year students have a seamless transition into their college career.

The GEMS position provides meaningful peer-to-peer interactions, which may increase students' sense of belonging and connection to the institution (Kuh, 1993). Additionally, Saint Peter's University retains their orientation leaders through the fall semester to assist the first-year students in their social skill development. Concurrently, GEMS offer academic support (N. Decapua, personal communication, March 20, 2014). This approach provides a holistic experience for students because it offers a structured opportunity for first-year students in which orientation leaders focus on social integration and GEMS focus on students' academic success.

Commuter and Transfer Assistants at Drexel University. The Commuter and Transfer Student Engagement office at Drexel University employs paraprofessional staff to promote involvement and engagement in the community among commuter and transfer students (Drexel University Office of Campus Engagement, n.d.). Commuter assistants (CAs) and transfer assistants (TAs) help first-year students transition to life at the university. Their specific focus on the two subpopulations is an intentional effort to enhance commuter and transfer success in academic and cocurricular activities. CAs and TAs interact with commuter and transfer students through a variety of means, including individual meetings, e-mails, social media, and special programs and events. Specifically, CAs must participate in Commuter Connection Day and TAs must participate in Transfer Student Orientation to connect with new students and promote campus and community services and resources. In order to be qualified for the CA or TA positions, applicants must have a minimum 2.50 GPA and have been a commuter or transfer student, respectively. The Office of Commuter and Transfer Student Engagement prepares the peer mentors through a summer training session and subsequent developmental workshops, retreats, and other in-service opportunities.

Drexel's peer mentor positions focus on the unique needs of the commuter and transfer subpopulations. There is a clear emphasis on student engagement as it relates to academic success; for example, these peer mentors maintain regular communication with mentees through meetings, phone calls, and e-mail, and assist students in becoming involved and meeting others within their community (Drexel University Office of Campus Engagement, n.d.). By attempting to alleviate the stressors accompanying the transition to a new institution (Astin, 1984), the peer mentor role may contribute to a positive first-year experience. This ideally results in integration into the institution and then likely yields student persistence (Tinto, 1986), which benefits both the student and the institution.

Peer Mentors at Paradise Valley Community College. Through the Counseling Division at Paradise Valley Community College (PVCC), peer mentors are hired to work with students in their required first-year College Success class or in developmental reading, English, or math classes and provide guidance and support to first-year students (Paradise Valley Community College, n.d.). Specifically, peer mentors are responsible for facilitating student engagement and positive relationships in class and out of the classroom by referring students to appropriate campus resources. In order to be eligible for the peer mentor position, students must participate in a Peer Mentor Training class during their first semester as peer mentors, which coaches them on topics like verbal and nonverbal skills, leadership styles, group facilitation skills, ethics, and challenges facing first-year college students. Applicants must have completed 24 credits, have a 3.00 GPA or better, be nominated or request nomination by a faculty member, and be given permission to participate in the leadership position through the Counseling Division (M. Auten, personal communication, June 5, 2014). This leadership opportunity allows students who serve as peer mentors to earn points toward the completion of an optional leadership certificate, develop their leadership skills, and enjoy the support of other community leaders.

PVCC's peer mentor program is interesting because it occurs at a two-year community college setting where it can be challenging to engage students in the absence of a residential program (Astin, 1984). These peer mentors are the students' link to learning outside of the classroom. This leadership position helps contribute to the student culture at PVCC so that both mentors and the students with whom they work feel connected to their institution (Kuh, 1993).

Academic Success Mentors at Indiana University of Pennsylvania. Within the Office of Housing, Residential Living, and Dining at Indiana University of Pennsylvania, academic success mentors (ASMs) are used to assist specific residential students (e.g., transfer students, academically at-risk students, and so on) with their educational goals and academic success (Indiana University of Pennsylvania Office of Housing, Residential Living, & Dining, 2014). ASMs foster student development through one-on-one meetings with assigned mentees, educational programming, and support of the living-learning programs within the community.

In order to be eligible for the ASM position, students must have at least a 2.75 GPA, submit an application, and participate in a group process interview. Although ASMs do not have to live on campus, their mentees are all residential students. ASMs participate in two weeks of training at the end of the summer, where they practice skill building related to their job responsibilities, such as effective communication and addressing challenges associated with first-year students. ASMs learn from a wide variety of campus and community resources, from peer advisors to the Office of International Education. Once hired, ASMs are expected to be knowledgeable about campus academic procedures, work collaboratively with other ASMs and community assistants (the student staff role comparable to a resident assistant), maintain records of mentee meetings, and hold programs that meet the needs of the residential community. ASMs are compensated as student employees for 20 hours of work per week, which includes office hours, staff meetings, supervision meetings, mentee meetings, and programs.

As is evident from the previously described mentor roles, many of these positions have common goals, expectations, hiring criteria, and so on. Similar elements exist for peer mentors working specifically with learning communities. Given that learning communities are intentionally structured to offer both learning and community support, including peer mentors as part of the program's staffing structure is advantageous. The specific goals and structural elements of the learning community provide guidance for the work of these student staff members. Often these elements are familiar to the peer mentors as applicants may be required to have participated as learning community members prior to employment. The following section offers examples of peer mentor roles that are specific to learning community programs.

Learning Community Peer Mentor Programs

Descriptions of a sample of peer mentor roles situated within the context of learning community programs are provided here.

Peer Mentors at Wayne State University. Learning communities at Wayne State University are small groups of students with similar interests who take classes together and live together (Wayne State University, 2014). Upper division student mentors and faculty advisors are involved in these communities to help students learn, study, and socialize together. The various learning community programs rely on the work of undergraduate peer mentors to be successful. The primary responsibility for peer mentors involves student interaction, such as developing individual and group relationships with the learning community students, communicating with assigned students in person and online, attending classes, and facilitating study groups together (Wayne State University, 2014). Peer mentors also have administrative responsibilities, which include maintaining records on student interactions and communicating student progress and concerns to their faculty advisors. For students to be eligible for the peer mentor position, they must be juniors or seniors with a minimum 3.00 GPA, possess knowledge of the course(s) related to the specific learning community program, and submit at least two references who can attest to their interpersonal skills, attitude, and work ethic. Once selected for the position, peer mentors must attend a two-day training that helps the student leaders set goals for their communities, understand the importance of diversity in their work, and learn about beneficial campus resources and tools. Beyond the training sessions, peer mentors are provided with a handbook that outlines various skills to succeed as a mentor, common issues for peer mentors, and lists of campus resources and services for students. Wayne State University's peer mentor program provides a standard example of peer mentor roles in learning communities.

Peer Mentors at East Tennessee State University. Within the East Tennessee State University (ETSU) Department of Housing and Residence Life, under the direction of the Assistant Director for Academic Initiatives, peer mentors (PMs) are used to provide leadership within the living-learning communities (East Tennessee State University Department of Housing and Residence Life, 2013a). At ETSU, living-learning communities are defined as residential communities for students who share common interests and passions in which members of the faculty and staff partner with PMs to enhance students' on-campus experience (East Tennessee State University Department of Housing and Residence Life, 2013b). PMs are live-in student staff members who work collaboratively with the Resident Advisors to develop a community focused on student success. Specifically, PMs are responsible for advocating academic success, promoting student engagement, and assisting with connecting students on campus with faculty, staff, and other students. They do this by providing weekly/monthly events focused on the community's learning outcomes, advising and referring as necessary, and serving as a role model, among other duties (East Tennessee State University Department of Housing and Residence Life, 2013a). In order to be eligible for the PM position, students must have a 3.00 GPA or higher and knowledge of or experience in the learning community. PMs are selected based on their application, experience, individual interview, references, and a background check. PMs develop their skills through specific PM training before the beginning of the fall semester and throughout the year. Once hired, PMs are expected to establish and maintain positive relationships with students, provide weekly activities/programs, act as a liaison between students and faculty/staff, and connect students to academic and social resources on campus to benefit the members of the community. The PMs are compensated $1,600 for their work throughout the academic year.

The PM position highlights the university's values by treating others with dignity and respect, building relationships, achieving excellence, and demonstrating commitment to intellectual achievement (East Tennessee State University Office of the ETSU President, n.d.). Additionally, PMs encourage student engagement throughout campus by coordinating regular activities and programs that align with the learning community's objectives to help students connect with peers, faculty, and staff. This integration of academic affairs with the residence hall environment may influence student learning and development.

Mount Leadership Society Scholars at Ohio State University. The Mount Leadership Society Scholars Program at Ohio State University is a learning community for students committed to leadership and community service (Ohio State University Honors & Scholars, 2013). Through the Office of Student Life, this program welcomes a class of 100 new students who live, attend leadership training meetings, take a one-credit seminar class, and complete service projects together. The peer mentoring within the Mount Leadership Society Scholars Program is called the "mini–mega" program, with first-year scholars referred to as the "minis" and second- and third-year scholars as the "megas." Each mini is assigned a mega, who is in communication even before the start of the academic year. The mega is a contact person who answers any questions and assists in the mini's transition to college. When the first-year students arrive on campus, their relationship with their mentors is further fostered through mini–mega events ranging from acclimation to campus with Launch Week to other social events, like retreats, service projects, and Mount Legacy Week. To remain eligible for the program, scholars must participate in all Mount Leadership Society activities, maintain a 3.00 or higher GPA, and demonstrate leadership and service in their work.

The mini–mega program values the one-to-one relationships formed between the mentors and the first-year students. This encourages the mentors to role model appropriate behavior for the community and share their knowledge and experiences with their protégés (Minor, 2007; Schmidt as cited in Merriam, 1983). The students live together in the community, which sets the environment for a common focus on leadership and service learning.

Important Elements in Peer Mentor Positions

This chapter examined several distinctly different peer mentor programs from institutions across the country. Although peer mentor programs are rapidly expanding, the research has not kept pace (Gershenfeld, 2014). It may be difficult to standardize the mentor role because different programs have significantly different needs. Despite these variations, this section attempts to highlight important elements existing in the aforementioned programs to provide common practices for those considering developing peer mentor programs.

Qualifications. There are certain qualities that make a good peer mentor. Newton and Ender (2010) identified several valuable characteristics, such as leadership, strong interpersonal communication skills, and relevant knowledge. In the higher education setting, it is important that peer mentors show evidence of academic strengths, often demonstrated by a strong GPA. Many programs have a GPA requirement of 2.50 or higher. Because students typically rise to the challenges presented to them by educators (Blake, 2007; Kuh, 1999), if educators establish high academic expectations for leadership roles such as the peer mentor position, students may push themselves to achieve in order to be eligible for these desirable roles. As such, these peer mentor programs should raise their GPA requirements beyond a 2.50 to raise the standard for this leadership role. Further support of academic integrity is often demonstrated through an endorsement from a faculty or staff member in the form of a reference (Minor, 2007). Beyond the academic component, it is important for students to share their experiences with one another. For many learning community programs, prior involvement in the learning community is a requirement to become a peer mentor in that community. This allows mentors to use past experiences to help their mentees. Valuable experiences as learning community members as well as information gained by observing and interacting with the peer mentors who guided them can provide important contextual information to guide the work of the peer mentors in the learning community (Benjamin, 2007).

Responsibilities and Expectations. Whether the peer mentor role is a paid or volunteer position, the students who serve as peer mentors have various responsibilities, and it is recommended that a written job description be provided to peer mentors prior to them beginning their work (Benjamin, 2007). Most universal is the expectation that mentors will engage with their mentees to help them transition to and become involved within the community. This student engagement looks different in various positions, including one-on-one student meetings, programs and events, and group socials. A secondary responsibility is one that involves personal and professional development. Peer mentors are expected to undergo training in the week(s) prior to the start of the academic year through a leadership development class or through ongoing retreats or workshops. This focus on development helps mentors refine important life skills (i.e., interpersonal, communication, helping, intervention, and so on) that can help them beyond the scope of their positions. Connecting the peer mentor position to other resources, specifically referral resources in the campus and community that they and other students would find beneficial, can further support leadership development. Ongoing supervision such as individual meetings with supervisors and program staff meetings are also important components to student mentors' development (Gershenfeld, 2014). Ultimately, this personal and professional development will help peer mentors and students who utilize their services benefit from the peer mentor role.

In each of the described peer mentor programs, there was the expectation that both the mentors and the mentees were benefiting from the relationship. For college students undergoing significant development, it is important that the peer mentor programs foster relationships that are structured to help both students involved (Jacobi, 1991). In order for the mentor relationships to be effective, they should maintain a manageable mentor–mentee ratio (Gershenfeld, 2014). That expectation might vary from institution to institution, but the ratio must be conducive to frequent contact. This mentoring structure is best sustained when the length of the mentoring relationship is a full academic year because the mentors can have an impact on the mentees, and then the mentees can pay that forward by becoming mentors themselves. As noted in a study of residential learning community peer mentors (Benjamin, 2007), learning community participants may become peer mentors because they had an exceptional mentor and they want to emulate that experience for others, or they may choose the peer mentor role because they believe they can provide better assistance than they received as learning community participants.

Conclusion

Peer mentor roles can be valuable to the students in the learning community, the coordinator of the learning community, and the peer mentors themselves due to the experiential education they receive by serving in this role. Relevant research supports the inclusion of peer mentor programs in a higher education setting, as they have the potential to add academic and social value to the college student experience. This chapter highlights examples of general peer mentor roles and those more specific to learning community programs. The authors offered several recommendations that can standardize peer mentor roles, while recognizing that peer mentor roles vary to serve the unique needs of the specific student population, learning community, or institution. This information may be useful in creating or improving peer mentor positions and contributing to a more universal understanding of what peer mentors do and why they are so useful.

References

Astin, A. W. (1984). Student involvement: A developmental theory for higher education. *Journal of College Student Development*, *25*, 226–236.

Benjamin, M. (2007). Role construction of residential learning community peer mentors. *Journal of College and University Student Housing*, *34*(2), 31–42.

Blake, J. H. (2007). The crucial role of student affairs professionals in the learning process. In E. L. Moore (Ed.), *New Directions for Student Services: No. 117. Student affairs staff as teachers* (pp. 65–72). San Francisco, CA: Jossey-Bass.

Colvin, J. W., & Ashman, M. (2010). Roles, risks, and benefits of peer mentoring relationships in higher education. *Mentoring & Tutoring: Partnership in Learning*, *18*(2), 121–134.

Drexel University Office of Campus Engagement. (n.d.). *Commuter and Transfer Assistants*. Retrieved from http://www.drexel.edu/studentaffairs/get_involved/commuter_transfers/Commuter%20and%20Transfer%20Assistants/

East Tennessee State University Department of Housing and Residence Life. (2013a). *Living-learning community peer mentor position information*. Retrieved from http://www.etsu.edu/students/housing/Department%20of%20HousingPeer%20Mentor.pdf

East Tennessee State University Department of Housing and Residence Life. (2013b). *Living-learning communities*. Retrieved from http://www.etsu.edu/students/housing/llc.aspx

East Tennessee State University Office of the ETSU President. (n.d.). *ETSU values*. Retrieved from http://www.etsu.edu/president/mission.aspx

Gershenfeld, S. (2014). A review of undergraduate mentoring programs. *Review of Educational Research*, *84*(3), 365–391. doi:10.3102/0034654313520512

Indiana University of Pennsylvania Office of Housing, Residential Living, & Dining. (2014). *Become an Academic Success Mentor*. Retrieved from http://www.iup.edu/newsItem.aspx?id=139963&blogid=691

Jacobi, M. (1991). Mentoring and undergraduate academic success: A literature review. *Review of Educational Research*, *61*(4), 505–532.

Kuh, G. D. (Ed.). (1993). *Cultural perspectives in student affairs work*. Washington, DC: American College Personnel Association.

Kuh, G. D. (1999). Setting the bar high to promote student learning. In G. S. Blimling, E. J. Whitt, & Associates (Eds.), *Good practice in student affairs: Principles to foster student learning* (pp. 67–89). San Francisco, CA: Jossey-Bass.

Merriam, S. (1983). Mentors and protégés: A critical review of the literature. *Adult Education Quarterly*, *33*(3), 161–173.

Miller, J. E., Groccia, J. E., & Miller, M. S. (2001). Introduction. In J. E. Miller, J. E. Groccia, & M. S. Miller (Eds.), *Student-assisted teaching: A guide to faculty-student teamwork* (pp. xv–xix). Bolton, MA: Anker.

Minor, F. D. (2007, fall). Building effective peer mentor programs [Monograph]. *Learning communities and student affairs: Partnering for powerful learning*, 1–13. Retrieved from http://www.evergreen.edu/washingtoncenter/about/monographs/lcsa.html

Newton, F. B., & Ender, S. C. (2010). *Students helping students: A guide for peer educators on college campuses* (2nd ed.). San Francisco, CA: Jossey-Bass.

Ohio State University Honors & Scholars. (2013). *Mount Leadership Society Scholars*. Retrieved from http://honors-scholars.osu.edu/scholars/programs/mount/about

Paradise Valley Community College. (n.d.). *Peer mentor program*. Retrieved from http://www.paradisevalley.edu/mentor

Pascarella, E. T., & Terenzini, P. T. (2005). *How college affects students: A third decade of research*. San Francisco, CA: Jossey-Bass.

Saint Peter's University First Year Experience. (2012). *GEMS peer mentor program*. Retrieved from http://www.saintpeters.edu/orientation/first-year-experience/gems-peer-mentor-program/

Sampson, J., & Cohen, R. (2001). Designing peer learning. In D. Boud, R. Cohen, & J. Sampson (Eds.), *Peer learning in higher education: Learning from and with each other* (pp. 21–34). London, UK: Kogan Page Limited.

Tinto, V. (1986). Theories of student departure revisited. In J. C. Smart (Ed.), *Higher education: Handbook of theory and research* (Vol. II, pp. 359–384). New York, NY: Agathon Press.

Wayne State University. (2014). *Learning communities*. Retrieved from http://www.lc.wayne.edu/peer-mentors/index.php

LAURA JO RIESKE is a residence life coordinator at Towson University.

MIMI BENJAMIN is an assistant professor in the Student Affairs in Higher Education Department at Indiana University of Pennsylvania.

7

Although assessment has been an integral part of the development and expansion of learning communities, much of the assessment was focused on investigating student satisfaction, retention, and graduation. This chapter provides a case study illustrating one learning community's efforts to create assessments focused on student learning.

Assessing the "Learning" in Learning Communities

Ann M. Gansemer-Topf, Kari Tietjen

The proliferation of learning communities (LCs) on college campuses suggests that these programs are worthwhile investments and, in many instances, have been held up as a symbol of "best practices" within higher education (Tinto, 2006). LCs have been designed to increase peer-to-peer interactions, student–faculty interactions, and engagement with the institution, all of which have been shown to improve retention, graduation, and academic progress (Pascarella & Terenzini, 2005; Zhao & Kuh, 2004). LCs are flexible and adaptable to most institutional environments: small, private liberal arts institutions; four-year large, public residential campuses; two-year community colleges; and brick and mortar as well as online environments (Lenning & Ebbers, 1999; Shapiro & Levine, 1999). They are also effective vehicles through which collaborative partnerships between student affairs and academic affairs are formed.

More broadly, LCs have become a symbol of an institution's commitment to student success. For example, in the past 10 years, *U.S. News and World Report* has published separate rankings based on "outstanding examples of academic programs that are believed to lead to student success" (*U.S. News and World Report*, n.d.). Institutions are annually ranked on their ability to provide exemplary programming, and LCs are an example of that programming. LCs became increasingly prevalent on college campuses in

Thank you to the PWSE staff for helping with the process of creating, implementing, and adjusting the OWLS process, including Lora Leigh Chrystal, Karen Zunkel, Carol Heaverlo, and Janice Crow. In particular, thank you to former graduate assistant Andrea Ramos-Lewis who was instrumental in conceiving the idea of the OWLS system as well as implementing it with LC peer mentors and students. Andrea, without your exceptional initiative and innovation, this work would not have happened.

the 1990s. At the same time that LCs were making their appearance, institutions, under increasing pressure to justify their costs and articulate their value, were beginning to focus more on assessment. The publication of Upcraft and Schuh's (1996) *Assessment in Student Affairs: A Guide for Practitioners* challenged student affairs professionals in particular to integrate assessment into their work. It is therefore not surprising that, at their onset, many LCs incorporated some form of assessment within their development. Institutions were willing to invest in these programs but were equally interested in knowing if this investment was worthwhile.

Much of the initial assessment on LCs was done for purposes of accountability. Accountability is focused on those stakeholders external to the institution—the public, government, policymakers. Data are primarily quantitative and used for reporting purposes or in benchmarking as a way to compare across institutions (Ewell, 2008). Rarely does this type of data get at the "why" or make specific suggestions for improvement (Blimling, 2013), but these types of data nevertheless were important in justifying an investment in resources. Other efforts would gauge students' levels of participation and satisfaction with their LC (see, e.g., Baker & Pomerantz, 2000; Johnson, 2000; Tinto, 1994), and data from these assessments could be used for both accountability purposes and program improvement. The results of these assessments have helped to secure LCs' place within institutions.

While a significant number of studies have focused on student outcomes related to LCs (see, for instance, Inkelas, 2008), many of these studies were measuring broader constructs such as critical thinking or civic engagement and subsequently compare LC members with those not in LCs. Few assessments focus specifically on the knowledge or concepts students learn during their LC experience. Ironically, although there is a great emphasis on developing a "learning" community, assessments often do not focus on the "learning" that takes place as a result of this participation (Bresciani, Gardner, & Hickmott, 2009; Huba & Freed, 2000). While measuring participation, satisfaction, retention, and graduation rates is important, another critical question arises: "What are students learning as a result of participating in a learning community?"

This chapter focuses on one LC that embarked on this assessment process. Having conducted previous assessments on student satisfaction and measuring retention and graduation rates, this LC refocused its efforts on developing learning outcomes and assessing students' performance on these outcomes. This case study serves as an example of how other LCs may engage in this process.

Program for Women in Science and Engineering: An Example of Measuring the Learning in a Learning Community

The Program for Women in Science and Engineering (PWSE) at Iowa State University (ISU) supports LCs for first-year, sophomore, and transfer females in science, technology, engineering, and mathematics (STEM) fields. Learning outcomes were implemented to guide programming provided by student peer mentors for LC students, as well as assessment measures conducted by PWSE staff. This initiative places emphasis on student learning and effective programming within LCs.

Program for Women in Science and Engineering Description. The PWSE has 12 first-year LCs as well as two sophomore and one transfer LC for females in STEM fields, which are traditionally male-dominated disciplines (National Science Foundation, 2013). PWSE is housed under ISU's Learning Communities program as well as the Office of the Provost. The program supports women in over 50 STEM majors at the university. ISU is a large, public institution located in the Midwest. Its undergraduate student population is just over 25,000, of which 44% are female (Iowa State University Office of the Registrar, 2013). At ISU, women were represented in the College of Engineering at 15% as compared to men for fall 2012 enrollment, a percentage that did not increase from fall 2011 (Iowa State University Office of the Registrar, 2013). While the representation of women varies by college and major, the number of women in engineering is an example of the historic underrepresentation of women that made necessary the creation of PWSE as a support system for women in male-dominated fields (Iowa State University Program for Women in Science and Engineering, 2012). PWSE aims to provide programs and opportunities, and to share knowledge of best practices for women in STEM education (Iowa State University Program for Women in Science and Engineering, 2012). PWSE lists six core values in its mission including (a) valuing people as individuals, (b) integrity and accountability, (c) inclusion, (d) collaboration, (e) leadership, and (f) excellence in all the PWSE graduate assistants do (Iowa State University Program for Women in Science and Engineering, 2012).

The program has a half-time director, two full-time staff members including the on-campus programs coordinator and the outreach coordinator, two half-time graduate assistants, and one three-quarter time support staff member. While the director and full-time staff are responsible for overseeing the entire program, the graduate assistants work directly with the peer mentors to provide programming for the PWSE participants.

The LCs serve almost one quarter (23%) of STEM women at ISU. The first-year PWSE programs, which are residentially based, include approximately 300 women and 12 peer mentors. LCs for sophomore and transfer students include three peer mentors and engage approximately 120 students. The core components of the sophomore and transfer LC experience include the interaction with a peer mentor as well as out-of-class field-related experiences. The sophomore LC is nonresidentially based while the transfer LC has an optional residential component; also, all students may elect to take a 1-credit course as part of the LC. While the sophomore and transfer LCs do not fit traditional models, at ISU this type of participation is considered an LC experience (Iowa State University Learning Communities, 2012).

Creation and Implementation of Outcomes. While PWSE staff and peer mentors had been tracking the retention of students in the LCs, there was no programming model or assessment specifically focused on student learning. Women in LCs were found more likely to be retained than women not in LCs (Iowa State University Program for Women in Science and Engineering, 2008), but assessment was not being done to understand what students learned or what specific elements may contribute to this increased retention. In realizing this void, two PWSE graduate assistants worked to introduce a set of learning outcomes. The intent was that these outcomes would guide peer mentors in creating programming and would provide the basis for subsequent assessment.

The Department of Residence at ISU created and was using a programming model based on five learning outcomes: academic skills, personal skills, understanding and appreciation of differences, leadership skills, and civic and community responsibility (Iowa State University Department of Residence, 2012). This model, the Living, Learning, Leading (LLL) model, was used by hall directors and community advisors (CAs) to guide their interactions with residents whether through conversations or passive or active programming.

Using the LLL model as a framework, the PWSE graduate assistants created a list of outcomes appropriate for the women in the PWSE LCs. As Suskie (2009) described, learning outcomes are a values statement of what we want our students to learn and why. The departmental mission and vision as well as feedback from past participants were used to guide learning outcome development. From these discussions, a set of outcomes was created based on four categories: academic/professional skills, understanding and appreciating human differences, leadership skills, and personal skills. Each of these main categories included three to seven specific outcomes that described specific "knowledge, skills, attitudes, and habits of mind" (Suskie, 2009, p. 117) that PWSE intended for women to gain from their learning experience in the LC (Table 7.1). These outcomes, entitled "Outcomes for Women in Leadership and STEM" (OWLS), were then used to create a future assessment plan and programming. By using weekly written submissions from the peer mentors about how they were working with students to achieve the learning outcomes and through pre- and posttest surveys of LC participants, the PWSE graduate assistants were able to assess the interactions between peer mentors and their students and identify programs that would assist students in meeting the learning outcomes.

Weekly Submissions From Peer Mentors. Each week peer mentors documented two interactions that they had with LCs' participants that directly related to the desired outcomes. Mentors were each required to submit notes to their supervisors from in-person conversations, emails, programs they held (active or passive), classroom interactions, or other creative

Table 7.1. Outcomes for Women in Leadership and STEM (OWLS) 2012–2013 (Iowa State University Program for Women in Science and Engineering, 2012)

Program for Women in Science and Engineering—OWLS	
Academic/ Professional Skills	*Outcomes*
AS1	PWSE women will be aware of campus resources that support academic success, especially for STEM majors.
AS2	PWSE women will develop an academic success plan (four-year plan).
AS3	PWSE women will demonstrate the ability to self-manage their study habits and time.
AS4	PWSE women will be able to identify individual and collaborative study techniques/skills that best support their ability to learn as women in STEM.
AS5	PWSE women will have an understanding of possible career paths for their chosen or potential major of study.
AS6	PWSE women will be prepared for career fairs, internships, interviews, etc.
AS7	PWSE women will know how to utilize social media for professional purposes and understand the impact of their online presence.
Understanding and Appreciating Human Differences	*Outcomes*
UAHD1	PWSE women will be able to develop strategies that will assist them to have conversations with people who are different from them.
UAHD2	PWSE women will be aware of campus resources that inform and educate on matters of diversity.
UAHD3	PWSE women will develop strategies and articulate the benefits of living and learning in an inclusive and diverse educational environment.
UAHD4	PWSE women and staff will be active participants in confronting behaviors that marginalize PWSE women and will actively combat the bystander effect.
UAHD5	PWSE women will be aware of issues facing women in STEM and have the skills to navigate environments where they are a minority.
Leadership Skills	*Outcomes*
LS1	PWSE women will demonstrate organizational and planning skills.
LS2	PWSE women will be aware of and participate in leadership opportunities.
LS3	PWSE women will be prepared to serve as campus and community leaders.

(*Continued*)

Table 7.1. Continued

Program for Women in Science and Engineering—OWLS	
Personal Skills	*Outcomes*
PS1	PWSE women will recognize and/or utilize resources that promote physical and mental health.
PS2	PWSE women will actively engage and socialize with other PWSE women and women in STEM.
PS3	PWSE women will identify a sense of identity, self-esteem, self-efficacy, confidence, and integrity.
PS4	PWSE women will recognize resources and practice effective decision making concerning their relationships.
PS5	PWSE women will take necessary precautions to ensure their personal safety.
PS6	PWSE women will develop positive methods for addressing stress.

interactions that emphasized a particular outcome. For example, one peer mentor submitted the following to show how her mentees were working toward Academic Skills 5 ("Women in Science and Engineering will have an understanding of possible career paths for their chosen or potential major of study."):

> On Thursday, I took three Civil Engineering women on a job shadow with my Structures Professor... Two of the three women are interested in emphasizing in structures, so it was great for them to get to see what an actual professional does. All three of the women expected Travis to design bridges since that's the first thing that comes to mind as a structural engineer; however, Travis tests the stresses and strains on bridges using strain gauges and analyzing the data. The women were very interested in this because they had no idea that bridge testing was an option.

Each mentor's submissions were unique to how she interpreted the outcomes, but all mentors were encouraged to rethink their mentor position in terms of how they achieved the OWLS with their students.

Pretest Survey. An online survey was sent in early September to all LC students (approximately 400 women) as a way to gather students' self-assessment and knowledge of the PWSE learning outcomes. The survey responses were used to develop programming and interventions that would improve student learning in each of the outcomes. As a part of the survey, students also created a distinctive code that respected their anonymity but also allowed staff to pair data from this pretest survey to a later posttest survey.

By disaggregating the data by classification (first-year, sophomore, transfers), the PWSE graduate assistants were able to distribute data to the staff of student peer mentors working with that specific classification of students as well as PWSE central staff to address main concerns for the women in the LCs generally. For example, data from the initial survey showed that among first-year participants, 54% said that they strongly disagreed or disagreed with the following statement: "I would feel prepared to attend the Career Fair and talk with potential employers." These data suggested that programs preparing students to interview or navigate the employment process would be useful. Other responses showed the need for discussion of academic resources, healthy behaviors, resources on campus, and discussion of the issues that face women in STEM. The information provided by the pretest survey was used to assist the peer mentors as they began to provide programs and activities for their students. Peer mentors were encouraged to return to the information provided by the survey if they were unsure of areas on which to focus throughout the year.

Posttest Survey. The posttest survey was sent out in mid-April of the spring 2013 semester to all LC participants with the aim of pairing pretest survey data with posttest survey data. The posttest survey, similar to the pretest survey, directly addressed the outcomes along with student knowledge and behavior. A total of 126 LC students began the posttest survey, with 111 completing the survey (88% completion rate). A total of 20 students completed both the pre- and posttest, as determined by the unique code each student provided. The small number of students that completed both the pre- and posttest data suggested that additional incentives should be used in the following year to increase this number. Rather than solely focusing on those who took both the pre- and posttest, data were pulled from all 111 students who completed the posttest survey to assess student knowledge and behavior at the end of the academic year as compared to the pretest survey. For example, students again were asked in the posttest survey to rate their agreement with the following statement: "I would feel prepared to attend the Career Fair and talk with potential employers." In the spring 2013 survey, 70% of all first-year students who completed the posttest survey either agreed or strongly agreed that they would be prepared to meet with employers, an increase of 27% from the fall survey. Programming was created specifically to enable the first-year students to feel prepared to attend the Career Fair based on the data received from the pretest survey. The goal of providing specific Career Fair programming was for students to feel better prepared for the Career Fair when we asked them the same question in the spring.

Adjusting the Outcomes. After the first semester using the OWLS system, the PWSE graduate assistants met to evaluate the outcomes. The PWSE graduate assistants added an outcome about social media and online presence, and removed several outcomes that seemed repetitive as a result of student feedback. This process of revisiting the outcomes occurred again at the end of the spring 2013 semester and will continue annually.

The PWSE graduate assistants also felt it was important to gather feedback from the peer mentors about the implementation of the OWLS. The peer mentors were using the outcomes to guide their interactions with mentees, so the PWSE graduate assistants sent an online survey to ask peer mentors for feedback on the OWLS. Peer mentors were asked about the ease of use of outcomes in their job, whether they felt like the outcomes provided peer mentors direction in how to program, and whether mentors felt as though the outcomes led students to learn in outlined areas. Peer mentors provided mixed reviews. While several saw their usefulness, others felt the outcomes were too rigid and felt as though they limited their work. Through both student input as well as input from PWSE staff, the implementation of the OWLS continues to evolve so that these outcomes become more effective indicators of student learning.

Assessment Lessons Learned. There are several lessons to be learned from the process of creating, implementing, and adjusting the OWLS system. First, don't wait until you feel like you have assessment "figured out" to begin assessing student learning. The PWSE graduate assistants began with an introductory knowledge of assessment and implemented a system that has revolutionized the department. Begin with discussions of what you want to assess and then create a system to highlight student learning. If you find that your assessments aren't telling you what you need to know, adjust and try again. As Schuh and associates (2009) have suggested, it is not important to strive for perfection, but aim for good enough.

Secondly, view assessment as a cycle and an iterative process (Maki, 2012). If the outcomes and assessments you have created don't seem to be "working," begin to reevaluate and adjust the process. An essential component of any effective assessment system is openness to feedback from stakeholders. Using feedback from students, staff, and others, adjust your processes regularly to further improve your assessment of student learning.

Finally, be prepared to share the assessment that is being done with other stakeholders. The outcomes created were shared with the PWSE Advisory Board in both the fall of 2012 and spring of 2013 to gain feedback about areas of focus for the program. In the future, assessment results will be shared with the Advisory Board to share the student learning in the LCs. Gaining approval from the Institutional Review Board (IRB) early in the process will help if you want to share your results within and outside of the institution. PWSE gained IRB approval for the OWLS pretest and posttest surveys before completing the assessments. This approval subsequently allowed PWSE the ability to share results at the institutional, regional, and national conference level. By preparing to share this information beforehand, the PWSE LCs and the OWLS system can be used to help other departments (at ISU and elsewhere) build systems that demonstrate student learning.

While the implementation of the OWLS system helps to indicate student learning in the PWSE LCs, future action is necessary to improve the OWLS. In addition, the PWSE department learned several lessons from its first year implementing the OWLS and will continue learning and improving the outcomes and assessment. For example, after speaking with the peer mentors about the outcomes, PWSE graduate assistants learned "less is more" when it comes to the number of outcomes used. Rather than using numerous outcomes that may emphasize similar points, paring down the outcomes to be user friendly was necessary. Having fewer, but broader outcomes increased the likelihood that outcomes will be measured. Too many outcomes, while providing more specificity, have the consequence of overwhelming and potentially paralyzing the assessment activities. Insight gained from others using the assessment will continue to be used to adjust the assessment process.

While the first year of implementation of the outcomes was a learning year, PWSE has now integrated the outcomes into its departmental culture. Assessment of the LCs at various levels, such as peer mentor feedback, surveys, focus groups of students, etc., is becoming further emphasized as the department hopes to demonstrate student learning.

Conclusion

This case study illustrates one way that LC coordinators can assess what students learn as a result of their participation in an LC. While it is ideal to incorporate learning outcomes at the onset of the program, it is also not too late to undertake this task with well-established LCs. In fact, this process may provide additional insights into the LC's effectiveness or illustrate previously overlooked areas that need improvement.

The case study also highlights challenges in conducting learning outcomes assessments for LCs. For instance, while social media and other interactive technologies have become commonplace among current college students, our learning outcomes or even definitions of LCs have been slow to incorporate these avenues of engagement. Students are spending more time online and yet our assessments still tend to focus on measuring the impact of students' face-to-face or physical participation in a program. Students are quick to use their cell phones to text, tweet, Instagram, and Facebook as a way to express their opinions and "likes," but when given a survey specifically for this purpose, they ignore it. If the intent of LCs is to involve students within their institutions, assessment methods that efficiently capture the student experience and accurately reflect the ways in which students are involved are critical. In other words, we must not only rethink how LCs have evolved, but we must rethink how we can effectively assess this evolution.

In addition, the changing demographics of our college students require assessment methods that account for these differences. For example, do students from underrepresented groups benefit from LCs in ways similar to their White peers? Are there differences in the effectiveness of LCs due to income, first-generation student status, or distance from home? Since LCs may differ for subpopulations of students (Hotchkiss, Moore, & Pitts, 2006), assessment methods must intentionally investigate these potential differences. While LCs may be established programs within an institution, the students who participate in these programs and the broader higher education context are changing (see, e.g., Levine & Dean, 2012). Just as LCs have been adapted to meet the needs of current students, assessment methods too will need to be adapted to accurately capture and evaluate this learning. In other words, as we continue to strengthen LCs, we must also evaluate and improve our methods for understanding the learning that happens within our LCs.

References

Baker, S., & Pomerantz, N. (2000). Impact of learning communities on retention at a metropolitan university. *Journal of College Student Retention*, 2(2), 115–126.

Blimling, G. (2013). Challenges of assessment in student affairs. In J. H. Schuh (Ed.), *New Directions for Student Services: No. 142. Selected contemporary assessment issues* (pp. 5–14). San Francisco, CA: Jossey-Bass.

Bresciani, M. J., Gardner, M. M., & Hickmott, J. (2009). *Demonstrating student success: A practical guide to outcomes-based assessment of learning and development in student affairs*. Sterling, VA: Stylus.

Ewell, P. T. (2008). Assessment and accountability in America today: Background and context. In V. M. H. Borden & G. R. Pike (Eds.), *New Directions for Institutional Research: No. 2008(S1). Assessing and accounting for student learning: Beyond the Spellings Commission* (pp. 7–17). San Francisco, CA: Jossey-Bass.

Hotchkiss, J. L., Moore, R. E., & Pitts, M. M. (2006). Freshman learning communities, college performance, and retention. *Education Economics*, 14(2), 197–210.

Huba, M. E., & Freed, J. E. (2000). *Learner-centered assessment on college campuses: Shifting the focus from teaching to learning*. Boston, MA: Allyn and Bacon.

Inkelas, K. (2008). *National study of living-learning programs: 2007 report of findings*. Retrieved from http://drum.lib.umd.edu/bitstream/1903/8392/1/2007%20NSLLP%20Final%20Report.pdf

Iowa State University Department of Residence. (2012). *Living, learning, leading (LLL)*. Retrieved from http://www.housing.iastate.edu/life/leadership/lll

Iowa State University Learning Communities. (2012). *What is a learning community?* Retrieved from http://www.lc.iastate.edu/whatis.html

Iowa State University Office of the Registrar. (2013). *Enrollment statistics*. Retrieved from www.registrar.iastate.edu/enrollment

Iowa State University Program for Women in Science and Engineering (PWSE). (2008). *Retention data on WiSE first-year learning communities*. Retrieved from http://www.wise.iastate.edu/PDF/WiSERetention.pdf

Iowa State University Program for Women in Science and Engineering (PWSE). (2012). *Strategic plan 2012–2016*. Retrieved from http://www.wise.iastate.edu/strategicplan.html

Johnson, J. L. (2000). Learning communities and special efforts in the retention of university students: What works, what doesn't, and is the return worth the investment? *Journal of College Student Retention*, 2(3), 219–238.

Lenning, O. T., & Ebbers, L. H. (1999). *The powerful potential of learning communities: Improving education for the future* (ASHE-ERIC Higher Education Report, 26[6]). Washington, DC: Graduate School of Education and Human Development, The George Washington University.

Levine, A., & Dean, D. R. (2012). *Generation on a tightrope*. San Francisco, CA: Jossey-Bass.

Maki, P. L. (2012). *Assessing for learning: Building a sustainable commitment across the institution*. Sterling, VA: Stylus.
National Science Foundation. (2013). *Women, minorities, and persons with disabilities in science and engineering*. Retrieved from http://www.nsf.gov/statistics/wmpd/2013/tables.cfm
Pascarella, E., & Terenzini, P. (2005). *How college affects students: Findings and insights from twenty years of research. Vol. 2. A third decade of research*. San Francisco, CA: Jossey-Bass.
Schuh, J. H., & Associates. (2009). *Assessment methods for student affairs*. San Francisco, CA: Jossey-Bass.
Shapiro, N. S., & Levine, J. H. (1999). *Creating learning communities: A practical guide to winning support, organizing for change, and implementing programs*. San Francisco, CA: Jossey-Bass.
Suskie, L. (2009). *Assessing student learning: A common sense guide* (2nd ed.). San Francisco, CA: Jossey-Bass.
Tinto, V. (1994). Constructing educational communities: Increasing retention in challenging circumstances. *Community College Journal*, *64*(4), 26–29.
Tinto, V. (2006). Research and practice of student retention: What next? *Journal of College Student Retention: Research, Theory and Practice*, *8*(1), 1–19.
Upcraft, M. L., & Schuh, J. H. (1996). *Assessment in student affairs: A guide for practitioners*. San Francisco, CA: Jossey-Bass.
U.S. News and World Report. (n.d.). *Learning communities*. Retrieved from http://colleges.usnews.rankingsandreviews.com/best-colleges/rankings/learning-community-programs
Zhao, C. M., & Kuh, G. D. (2004). Adding value: Learning communities and student engagement. *Research in Higher Education*, *45*(2), 115–138.

ANN M. GANSEMER-TOPF is an assistant professor of higher education in the School of Education at Iowa State University.

KARI TIETJEN is currently a job developer with Candeo Iowa.

8

This chapter serves as a resource of recent learning community literature.

Learning Community Literature: Annotated Bibliography

Sarah Conte

This volume of *New Directions for Student Services* has discussed aspects of learning communities in great depth and detail. Topics like history, online education, transfer students, and methods of assessment, among others, are represented to provide further insight for professionals. However, as any student affairs practitioner can recognize, programs like learning communities are complex, ever-changing entities. New research will undoubtedly be required as new issues surface and new themes emerge. A broad review of available literature can inform future practice and forthcoming research subjects. With that in mind, below are additional resources to shed further light on the topics discussed in the chapters of this volume.

Annotated Bibliography

Benjamin, M. (2007). Role construction of residential learning community peer mentors. *Journal of College & University Student Housing*, *34*(2), 31–42.

This study hoped to identify noteworthy components of peer mentor role construction by analyzing documents and by conducting focus groups of residential learning community peer mentors at a large, public, research-intensive institution in the Midwest. Findings suggested that role construction began before the job commenced due to observing and reflecting upon the performance of the learning community peer mentors who assisted them as first-years. The peer mentors' perceptions of their roles were barely influenced by written documents, but peer mentors were receptive to verbal feedback from students enrolled in their learning communities. The article concluded with potential limitations of the study, as well as recommendations for professionals who work with residential learning community peer mentors.

Brower, A. M., & Inklas, K. K. (2010). Living-learning programs: One high-impact educational practice we now know a lot about. *Liberal Education*, 96(2), 1–9.

Retrieved from https://www.aacu.org/publications-research/periodicals/living-learning-programs-one-high-impact-educational-practice-we

The authors offered their expertise based on data collected through the National Study of Living-Learning Programs. They provided a history of living-learning programs, then explained the study and reported information based on participants from more than six hundred living-learning programs in the United States. Seventeen program themes emerged, as well as several structural trends. The authors addressed learning outcomes and benefits of participation, and then listed suggestions for professionals to consider when structuring a living-learning program.

Browne, M. N., & Minnick, K. J. (2005). The unnecessary tension between learning communities and intellectual growth. *College Student Journal*, *39*(4), 775–783.

The authors suggested that learning communities rarely or never focus on intellectual growth; therefore, they explained Integrating Moral Principles and Critical Thinking (IMPACT), a learning community designed to promote intellectual skills. They described the purpose of learning communities and mentioned a few specific programs, noting a lack of emphasis on critical thinking and moral reasoning in almost all communities they researched. Students who participated in IMPACT, however, self-reported high levels of satisfaction and scored higher on tests than other students.

Coston, C. T. M., Lord, V. B., & Monell, J. S. (2013). Improving the success of transfer students: Responding to risk factors. *Learning Communities Research and Practice*, *1*(1), Article 11. Retrieved from http://washingtoncenter.evergreen.edu/lcrpjournal/vol1/iss1/11

The authors discussed transfer students, their prevalence on community college campuses, and their unique difficulties—particularly higher departure rates. The criminal justice department at a large southeastern public university began that institution's first transfer student learning community by enrolling 15 students. These students identified personal stressors and, at three different times, rated the impact of the stressor. This exploratory study found that the leading influence on stress reduction was a feeling of belongingness.

DiRamio, D., & Wolverton, M. (2006). Integrating learning communities and distance education: Possibility or pipedream? *Innovative Higher Education*, *31*(2), 99–113. doi:10.1007/s10755-006-9011-y

The authors wondered if principles from successful learning communities could be used to evaluate the effectiveness of online courses. Issues like high attrition rates and questionable quality of content motivated their mixed-method electronic survey. Seventy-three respondents from a sample of attendees at a learning communities conference served as the basis for the authors' new diagnostic tool. They discovered that three specific factors found in learning communities—connections, experience, and responsibility—can be used as a framework to inform virtual classrooms and test their quality.

Domizi, D. P. (2008). Student perceptions about their informal learning experiences in a first-year residential learning community. *Journal of the First-Year Experience & Students in Transition*, *20*(1), 97–110.

Domizi conducted a qualitative study to discover what, if any, types of informal learning were taking place beyond the learning community's formal course objectives. Two group interviews were conducted with a total of six eighteen-year-old students, each of whom was a member of the education-themed learning community. The findings suggested that members of learning communities learned from each other by accommodating for personal differences and by noticing when interactions included them or excluded them.

Dunlap, L., & Pettitt, M. (2008, spring). Assessing student outcomes in learning communities: Two decades of study at community colleges. *Journal of Applied Research in the Community College*, *15*(2), 140–149.

The authors noticed a need for research about learning outcomes instead of simply tracking easily quantifiable data like retention and GPA, among others. They outlined the learning community model at their institution and described their initial assessment techniques. The authors then introduced five specific research initiatives that focused on student learning outcomes and discussed future opportunities for effective assessments. A review of two decades of data led them to conclude that students who participate in learning communities experience significant positive effects.

Dunn, M. S., & Dean, L. A. (2013). Together we can live and learn: Living-learning communities as integrated curricular experiences. *Schole: A Journal of Leisure Studies & Recreation Education*, *28*(1), 11–23.

This article considered living-learning communities as methods for facilitating both curricular and cocurricular learning within a living environment. The history of learning communities was delineated, and examples were provided. The authors highlighted assessment of learning communities by considering multiple theoretical frameworks for assessing student learning outcomes.

Firmin, M. W., Warner, S. C., Firmin, R. L., Johnson, C. B., & Firebaugh, S. D. (2013). Attitudinal outcomes of a multicultural learning community experience: A qualitative analysis. *Learning Communities Research and Practice*, *1*(1), Article 9. Retrieved from http://washingtoncenter.evergreen.edu/lcrpjournal/vol1/iss1/9

The authors argued that learning communities can be an effective platform for enhancing diverse interactions among students. They interviewed senior students who participated in a multicultural learning community at a small, private Midwestern university during their first year of college. Interviews revealed main findings, which included a shift in Caucasian students' personal biases and stereotypes, as well as a generally positive experience in the learning community among most students regardless of ethnic/racial background.

Garrett, M. D., & Zabriskie, M. S. (2004). The influence of living-learning program participation on student-faculty interaction. *Journal of College & University Student Housing*, *33*(1), 38–44.

The authors cited separate bodies of research regarding the effects of student–faculty interaction and the effects of living-learning communities, the majority of which were positive. They created a survey instrument to measure differences in student–faculty interaction between those students involved in a living-learning community and those who were not. The data showed that students who participated in living-learning communities were more likely to interact with faculty. The authors suggested further research regarding the quality of these interactions.

Gebauer, R. D., Watterson, N. L., Malm, E., Filling-Brown, M. L., & Cordes, J. W. (2013). Beyond improved retention: Building value-added success on a broad foundation. *Learning Communities Research and Practice*, *1*(2), Article 4. Retrieved from http://washingtoncenter.evergreen.edu/lcrpjournal/vol1/iss2/4

The living-learning communities (LLC) program at Cabrini College experienced great success, evidenced by increased retention and academic success among student participants. The authors sought to discover some of the LLCs' wider effects by observing individual student successes over time. They described the creation of a director position to coordinate the first-year experiences of the LLC and discussed how this director was able to engage faculty in shared purpose. The article concluded with a faculty reflection and a personal story from a student participant.

Goodsell Love, A. (2004, June). A campus culture for sustaining learning communities. In J. Levine Laufgraben & N. Shapiro (Eds.), *Sustaining and improving learning communities* (pp. 14–30). San Francisco, CA: Jossey-Bass.

Goodsell Love explained the important roles of organizational change and culture, as well as barriers that may surface when attempting to create a long-lasting learning community. She discussed aligning learning community purposes with institutional missions and goals, and she outlined the potential impacts of effective leaders. The author also suggested involving faculty and integrating the curriculum, in addition to emphasizing the need for ongoing assessment efforts.

Heaney, A., & Fisher, R. (2011). Supporting conditionally-admitted students: A case study of assessing persistence in a learning community. *Journal of the Scholarship of Teaching and Learning*, *11*(1), 62–78.

The authors explored factors that influenced persistence among conditionally admitted, first-year students in a learning community designed to offer them academic and social support. Using Astin's I–E–O model as a framework for the study, the authors distributed a 40-item survey to participating students. The survey found and focused on three influential concepts: social integration, academic integration and future goals, and self-regulated learning. The results informed policy decisions and caused the reconsideration of high-impact instructional approaches at the host university.

Hill, W., & Woodward, L. S. (2013). Examining the impact learning communities have on college of education students on an urban campus. *Journal of College Student Development*, *54*(6), 643–648.

The authors attempted to evaluate the impact of participation in a learning community on student retention. After collecting past and present data on students at an urban commuter university, the researchers compared this information to whether or not the students remained in higher education. They found that, in general, involvement in a learning community improved rates of student retention regardless of ethnicity or high school GPA.

Huerta, J. C., & Bray, J. J. (2013). How do learning communities affect first-year Latino students? *Learning Communities Research and Practice*, *1*(1), Article 5. Retrieved from http://washingtoncenter.evergreen.edu/lcrpjournal/vol1/iss1/5

Escalating enrollments of Latino students in American higher education led the authors to study how learning communities may affect Latino students compared to non-Hispanic White students. The project's data were obtained from a web-based survey of students in a first-year learning community at a designated Hispanic-Serving Institution in the southern United States. Results indicated that learning communities, especially those that emphasized collaborative learning, did in fact benefit Latino students, and not at the expense of other students.

Huerta, J. C., & Hansen, M. J. (2013). Learning community assessment 101—Best practices. *Learning Communities Research and Practice*, *1*(1), Article 15. Retrieved from http://washingtoncenter.evergreen.edu/lcrpjournal/vol1/iss1/15

This article reported on what the authors considered to be best practice for preparing to assess a learning community. The five tips included articulating goals, identifying the purpose of assessment, using mixed methods, considering direct and indirect measures of student learning, and ensuring that results are actually used when making decisions. Each of the five practices was explained and the authors provided a planning checklist for assessment.

Hughes, G. (2007). Diversity, identity and belonging in e-learning communities: Some theories and paradoxes. *Teaching in Higher Education*, *12*(5/6), 709–720. doi:10.1080/13562510701596315

Hughes wondered if issues of diversity and equality affect online learning environments as they do traditional learning environments. She discussed identity congruence, as well as inclusion versus exclusion, in the online learning arena. Hughes then recognized three inconsistencies that have led to inequitable participation in e-learning, including group identification, how much the students know about each other, and varying definitions of inclusion. She concluded by discussing potential ways to resolve these significant issues.

Inkelas, K., Daver, Z. E., Vogt, K. E., & Leonard, J. (2007). Living-learning programs and first-generation college students' academic and social transition to college. *Research in Higher Education*, *48*(4), 403–434.

The number of first-generation college students is increasing in the United States, and research proved that the transition to college can be especially difficult for this population. Data were collected at 33 institutions of higher education in order to study the role of living-learning programs in easing the academic and social transition to college for first-generation students. The findings suggested that participation in a living-learning program was beneficial for first-generation college students, as the programs seemed to provide positive transitions.

Jaffee, D. (2007). Peer cohorts and the unintended consequences of freshman learning communities. *College Teaching*, *55*(2), 65–71.

Due to a lack of research on the social–psychological dynamics of first-year learning communities (FLCs), Jaffee explored the unintended outcomes of FLCs on students' social lives. Informal data collection identified inadvertent consequences, including disorderly student behavior, student resistance to learning, and conflict between students and faculty. Jaffee concluded by recommending suggestions for how professionals who coordinate and/or teach FLCs can avoid the more negative consequences.

Jaffee, D., Carle, A. C., Phillips, R., & Paltoo, L. (2008). Intended and unintended consequences of first-year learning communities: An initial investigation. *Journal of the First-Year Experience and Students in Transition*, *20*(1), 53–70.

This article focused on the impact of first-year learning communities on students' social lives. A survey was distributed to students in three types of classes in order to discover if the intended and suspected unintended outcomes occurred and if the outcome was dependent upon the type of class. Sociological principles informed the authors as to which positive and negative consequences were possible. Survey results suggested that first-year learning communities fostered a sense of community but with both positive and negative aspects.

James, P. A., Bruch, P. L., & Jehangir, R. R. (2006). Ideas in practice: Building bridges in a multicultural learning community. *Journal of Developmental Education*, *29*(3), 10–18.

This article provided an operational definition of learning communities with special attention on the developmental benefits for students. The authors created an interdisciplinary learning community—focused on community, identity, and agency—that was composed of culturally diverse, first-generation student volunteers. The authors believed that students gained greater personal insight and improved academically. Data on persistence patterns were tracked for years following.

Jehangir, R. R. (2009). Cultivating voice: First-generation students seek full academic citizenship in multicultural learning communities. *Innovative Higher Education*, *34*(1), 33–49.

This study examined the impact of a learning community for first-year, first-generation college students that featured a multicultural curriculum which highlighted themes of identity, community, and social agency. The author quoted student participants' weekly written reflections to qualitatively describe their experiences. Five overarching themes emerged from the analysis of students' responses: bridge building, conflict as a catalyst, finding place, finding voice, and transformational learning. The author concluded by outlining potential implications for practice.

Levin Laufgraben, J. L., O'Connor, M. L., & Williams, J. (2007, fall). Supporting first-year transitions: Learning communities and educational reform. In B. L. Smith & L. B. Williams (Eds.), *Learning communities and student affairs: Partnering for powerful learning* (pp. 47–55). Olympia, WA: National Association of Student Personnel Administrators and the Washington Center for Improving the Quality of Undergraduate Education.

This chapter discussed how collaboration between faculty, academic affairs, and student affairs can increase student success through learning community programs. Seven characteristics of the authors' partnership were described, as these principles guided their professional practice. The authors concluded by explaining the effects of the partnership on the campus community and its impact beyond the learning communities program.

Maddix, M. A. (2013). Developing online learning communities. *Christian Education Journal*, *10*(1), 139–148.

Maddix defined traditional learning communities and discussed the reasons for and potential of online learning communities specifically at Christian-affiliated institutions. Those working in Christian higher education have been concerned about whether or not online learning communities can efficiently teach and influence students with regard to their faith and religion. The author presented arguments for and against online education as theological education, and listed enhancing factors and best practices of online learning communities.

Mino, J. (2013). Link aloud: Making interdisciplinary learning visible and audible. *Learning Communities Research and Practice*, *1*(1), Article 4. Retrieved from http://washingtoncenter.evergreen.edu/lcrpjournal/vol1/iss1/4

Mino focused on how students integrate their learning in interdisciplinary learning communities at a community college. He reviewed samples of student writing and verbal protocols—or recordings of students articulating their thinking processes—and identified 12 specific mechanisms of integration. Students in the learning community stated that the verbal protocol itself was a beneficial learning experience that led to significant personal discovery. Mino concluded by offering his own reflections on the quality of intellectual work submitted by participating students.

Nownes, N., & Stebleton, M. (2010). Reflective writing and life-career planning: Extending the learning in a learning community model. *Teaching English in the Two-Year College*, *38*(2), 118–131.

Nownes and Stebleton chronicled their collaboration as faculty members of a learning community that linked a life-career planning course with a composition course for first-semester students. The learning community, named "Exploring the World of Work through Reflective Writing," resulted from an extensive planning process among faculty—which the authors explained fully. The authors described content of both courses in detail, especially their multiple linked assignments. They explained how and why this learning community was a great success, and then concluded with suggestions for other faculty in similar situations.

Rocconi, L. (2011). The impact of learning communities on first year students' growth and development in college. *Research in Higher Education*, *52*(2), 178–193. doi:10.1007/s11162-010-9190-3

The author surveyed a sample of 241 first-year students at an urban research university to discover potential relationships between participating in a learning community, self-reported learning outcomes, and level of involvement. The article defined "learning community" and outlined some results of participation as a first-year student. The study used Pace's model of student development (1979, 1984) as a frame of reference. Results showed that participation in a learning community was indirectly linked to educational improvements because of student engagement.

Rodriguez, G. G., & Buczinsky, C. (2013). Linking classes: Learning communities, "high" culture, and the working class student. *Learning Communities Research and Practice*, *1*(2), Article 6. Retrieved from http://washingtoncenter.evergreen.edu/lcrpjournal/vol1/iss2/6

Two English professors from a small, Midwestern, urban, Catholic college reported on the institution's reformation of general education requirements to better serve their diverse and underprepared student body. They implemented a mandatory learning community—Humanities, Religion, and English Composition courses linked for first-year students—in the hopes that this restructuring would improve retention and increase student learning. Success was measured through retention data and a pretest/posttest questionnaire. The authors concluded that closely linked courses fostered the largest increase in student learning, while learning communities in general improved retention rates.

Schein, H. K. (2005, October). The zen of unit one: Liberal education at residential learning communities can foster liberal learning at large universities. In N. S. Laff (Ed.), *New Directions for Teaching and Learning: No. 103. Identity, learning, and the liberal arts* (pp. 73–88). San Francisco, CA: Jossey-Bass.

The long-term director of the Unit One Living-Learning Program at the University of Illinois, Urbana–Champaign described this unique, residentially based academic program. One of the many goals of Unit One was to offer students an experience similar to a small, liberal arts college although they were enrolled at a large, research-based university. Schein described the structure of the program, their methods of assessment, and the difference between student affairs professionals' and faculty members' philosophies of and involvement in learning communities. The article concluded with an overview of qualitative feedback from multiple constituents involved in this program.

Shapiro, N. (2013). When the students we have are not the students we want: The transformative power of learning communities. *Learning Communities Research and Practice*, *1*(1), Article 17. Retrieved from http://washingtoncenter.evergreen.edu/lcrpjournal/vol1/iss1/17

Shapiro, in her keynote address at the 12th Annual National Learning Communities Conference, suggested that the "magic ingredient" behind the most successful learning communities was the collaboration between academic affairs and student affairs. She provided demographic information about current college students and explored the many roles learning communities can fill on campuses across the country. She concluded with a call to action for student affairs professionals to document their learning community successes in order to provide evidence for the argument of collaboration.

Shultz, N. (2013). Learning communities as a first step in an integrative learning curriculum. *About Campus*, *18*(4), 26–29.

Shultz explained the unique approach taken by Arcadia University's learning community coordinators. They combined traditional learning community values with the belief that students should become engaged with the outside world as an additional learning environment. Shultz provided examples of content-related outings and reported that first-to-second-year retention increased. She described the helpful partnership between student affairs and academic affairs, and spoke highly of the effects the interactive experiences have on students and the campus.

Soldner, M., & Szelenyi, K. (2008). A national portrait of today's living-learning programs. *The Journal of College and University Student Housing*, *35*(1), 14–31.

The authors defined living-learning programs and introduced the reader to the National Study of Living-Learning Programs (NSLLP), which is a multiyear, multi-institutional study in its tenth year. A description of the demographics of the participating institutions followed, as well as a discussion of some main characteristics of living-learning programs, such as size, staffing, resources, and levels of funding. The article also explored some of the features related to the curriculum, including various activities, types of courses offered, and involvement levels of faculty and staff.

Tampke, D. R., & Durodoye, R. (2013). Improving academic success for undecided students: A first-year seminar/learning community approach. *Learning Communities Research and Practice*, *1*(2), Article 3. Retrieved from http://washingtoncenter.evergreen.edu/lcrpjournal/vol1/iss2/3

The authors studied outcomes of three groups of incoming students at a southern, public, research university: a group enrolled in a learning community that included a first-year seminar course, a group who enrolled in only the first-year seminar course, and a group who experienced neither. The authors explained their analysis, which focused on academic success outcomes like retention and GPA. The learning community produced the highest retention rates, while GPA was highest among the group in only the first-year seminar. The article concluded with a discussion of the study's limitations, as well as suggestions for practitioners.

Zhao, C., & Kuh, G. (2004). Adding value: Learning communities and student engagement. *Research in Higher Education*, *45*(2), 115–138.

This study questioned whether participating in a learning community affected student success and satisfaction. The authors randomly selected approximately 80,000 first-year and senior students from four-year institutions who completed the National Survey of Student Engagement (NSSE). By considering 47 items from the NSSE, they created scales to measure levels of student engagement, perceived quality of campus environment, and self-reported learning outcomes. Results showed that participation in a learning community is positively linked with students' overall satisfaction and academic performance.

SARAH CONTE is the assistant coordinator of the Academic and Career Success Center at Penn State New Kensington.

INDEX

OTHER TITLES AVAILABLE IN THE
NEW DIRECTIONS FOR STUDENT SERVICES SERIES
Elizabeth J. Whitt, Editor-in-Chief
John H. Schuh, Associate Editor

For a complete list of back issues, please visit www.wiley.com

SS148 ***Strategic Directions for Career Services Within the University Setting***
Kelli K. Smith
It is currently a "Golden Age" within the field of career services—heightened expectations, top-level attention, and university leadership looking for transformation. It is therefore critical for those within the profession and those making policy related to career services to understand its central importance. In this volume the authors provide an overview of emerging trends for career services and identify strategic directions and practical advice for the profession. Some of the topics include the following:

- a blend of research, case studies, and personal experiences that are intended to stimulate a productive dialogue about career services
- how career services professionals should be leaders in creating university-wide, innovative career programs and systems
- discussions of assessment, collaboration with academic advising, external relations, and internationalization

These topics are vitally important to practitioners and those in university leadership roles. Additionally, it is important for professionals within the field to remain current with strategic directions, learn from best practices, and have an opportunity to be the ones to "tell our story."
ISBN 978-11190-23845

SS147 ***Research-Driven Practice in Student Affairs: Implications From the Wabash National Study of Liberal Arts Education***
Georgianna L. Martin, Michael S. Hevel Editors
As student affairs units face increasing pressure to use data and evidence to inform planning and decisions, the research related to higher education has become more complex and, in some cases, less accessible. This issue of *New Directions for Student Services* aims to bridge this gap by drawing implications for student affairs programs and practices from the results of the Wabash National Study of Liberal Arts Education, an investigation that followed thousands of college students at more than 50 colleges and universities. The chapter authors identify research-based ways that student affairs practitioners can facilitate educational outcomes, including critical thinking, moral reasoning, and intercultural competence, while being sensitive to the needs of specific populations of students.
ISBN 978-11189-79556